D1561385

ESCAPE FROM TURKEY

Zeynep Kayadelen

Edited by Eyyup Esen

Zeynep Kayadelen

Author Zeynep Kayadelen was born in Cankiri, Turkey on August 16, 1972. From the very early stages of her life, Kayadelen knew that she had to be involved in the magical world of words. Even when she was only a toddler, she used to turn the pages of the books around and touch the letters to make some sense out of them.

When it was time, Kayadelen began attending elementary school with great enthusiasm and learned how to read and write so fast, just like a thirsty person who finally found water to drink. She started to write regularly, pretty much from the day she learned how to read and write. She had somehow sensed during early childhood that life is only made up of some contents and ideas which could be expressed using words. She felt as if there were other magnificent worlds inside her, and the magic key to those worlds were words. This was her driving motivation for reading and writing throughout her life.

Kayadelen attended middle and high school at Sinop Teacher Training School. During this time period, she received awards in several poetry and prose contests. In 1989, Kayadelen got admitted to the Department of Teaching in Primary Education at Abant University, however she didn't complete her studies because she preferred to devote herself entirely to research and writing. During the time she spent in the university, she regularly wrote articles for the college newspaper.

In her early career, she used to write more poetry. Later on, she mostly wrote novels and stories. Five of her novels have been published and printed in many editions in Turkey, namely *Reyhan, Yitik Mevsim, Alpdoğan, Kadim Sır,* and *Menekşe Günler.*

Kayadelen, enjoyed listening and writing tales because the intriguing atmosphere of the Eastern fairy tales had also rooted in her soul. As a result, she published two fairy tale books, *Adsız Oğlan ve Acayip Cüce (The nameless boy and the strange dwarf),* and *Örümcek Tüneli (The Spider Tunnel).*

For a long time, Kayadelen has received education in screenwriting, and has worked in this field. She was one of the three screenwriters who wrote the script of the animation movie Allah'ın Sadık Kulu (Barla), which was released in 2011. The movie was the first in its genre for Turkey and had its place in the 50 highest-grossing Turkish movies of all time. Kayadelen wrote scripts for several TV series, too.

Kayadelen's main goal in life was to make this world a more peaceful and prosperous place, both for herself and others. That's why volunteer work and charity have become a way of life for her.

After the so-called coup attempt on July 15, 2016, groundless accusations were made against Kayadelen. Her name had been added to the list of terrorists, among tens of thousands other innocent people. Her novels and story books had been banned and collected by the government. At the end, Kayadelen had to leave her beloved country without being able to take even one of her books.

After she escaped the darkness covering her homeland, she moved on to wherever she saw light and hope. Married with 5 children, she is now living in Toronto, Canada.

While she continues to write about many different projects, Kayadelen also feels the responsibility to write about the ongoing tragedies in Turkey.

Kayadelen believes in the power of peace and love. In her view, what the world needs is more love and compassion, regardless of whatever it is that the people are fighting for.

Eyyup Esen

Eyyup Esen was born and raised in Turkey. He received his BA in Turkish Language and Literature from Karadeniz Technical University in Turkey, his MA in Educational Studies from the University of Cincinnati and a second MA in Communication and Leadership from Park University. Esen earned his PhD in the Higher Education Administration from the University of Kansas in 2015. Also holding a Certificate in Peace Education, Esen is currently involved in the work of the Dialogue Institute, aka 'Movement of Global Warming of Hearts' in his own words. In addition, he is working as a college access advisor at Wichita State University. Esen is interested in establishing dialogue with people of different cultures and ethnicities. He also organizes a variety of events to promote peace and dialogue. His goal is to contribute to the global warming of hearts to depolarize the world. In 2014, Esen was presented the Most Outstanding International Student Award by the University of Kansas, which is only given to one graduate student in an academic year. In 2018, Esen published his first book with the title "Global Warming of Hearts!" His second book "I Am Not Color Blind" got published in 2020. Currently working as a volunteer at the Dialogue Institute of Kansas City, Esen is a human rights activist and an advisory board member of the Advocates of Silenced Turkey since 2020.

AST PUBLISHING

ESCAPE FROM TURKEY

www.silencedturkey.org
Published: 07/21
ISBN: 9798541026443

CONTENTS

We dedicate this work, which is based on a true story, to the thousands of people in Turkey, who have been deprived of their liberty and still face persecution. We dedicate it to the innocent people who had to flee their homeland and get separated from their families, to all victims who have set out for a new life in which they just want to live freely without further injustice, and to those who have lost all their hope of going back and living in their homeland.

We would like to thank everyone who has contributed to this book. Our sole wish is that the injustice, lawlessness, and victimization that many have been suffering from, will come to an end as soon as possible via the re-establishment of the rule of law.

ABOUT THE HIZMET MOVEMENT

Hizmet is a transnational civil society initiative that advocates for the ideals of human rights, equal opportunity, democracy, non-violence, and the emphatic acceptance of religious and cultural diversity. This widespread movement began in Turkey as a grassroots community in the 1970s in the context of social challenges being faced at the time: violent conflict among ideologically and politically driven youth, desperate economic conditions, and decades of a state-imposed ideology of discrimination that mandated a particular lifestyle.

Over the years, Hizmet has transformed from a grassroots community in Turkey to a wider global effort with participants from all walks of life. Their work is centered upon promoting philanthropy and community service, investing in education to cultivate virtuous individuals, organizing intercultural and interfaith dialogue events to promote more peaceful coexistence.

Hizmet participants are inspired by the ideas and example of Fethullah Gulen, a Muslim scholar who has expressed the belief that serving fellow humans is serving God.

For more information: www.afsv.org

EDITOR'S NOTE

Advocates of Silenced Turkey (AST) is a non-governmental organization that runs its activities on a voluntary basis. The aim of AST is to bring before international public opinion the human rights violations, including torture and the unlawful court trials and proceedings, which have been encountered in Turkey since 2018. After 2016, more than 160,000 innocent people lost their jobs in both public and private sectors, with accusations and unjust convictions of being connected with the coup attempt. The State of Emergency, which was announced on July 20, 2016, gave the government unchecked powers - in the disguise of combatting terrorism - to persecute thousands of people with no accountability and to undermine the fundamental principles of a democratic society and the most basic principles of universal human rights and values such as freedom of expression and freedom of the press. Today, tens of thousands of highly qualified professionals such as judges, prosecutors, doctors, teachers, journalists, academics, and military officers have been detained and imprisoned in Turkey due to bogus terrorism charges. Around 5,000 of them are women, along with nearly 345 children who stay with their mothers in prisons. These people have little or no hope of surviving the grueling atmosphere in Turkey, and as they are banned from leaving the country, they have no other choice but to flee at the risk of losing their lives by crossing the borders via dangerous routes. Some of them have not survived this difficult journey.

As the Advocates of Silenced Turkey, we engage in a number of activities in order not to keep silent about the injustices that have been taking place in Turkey where the rule of law has been suspended for a long time.

APH (Archiving the Persecution of Hizmet Movement) project of recording and archiving the testimonies of victims, aims to shed light on the injustices suffered by thousands of people in Turkey. Our volunteers have conducted hundreds of interviews and thanks to their efforts, the victimizations and hardships that the victims experienced are now being recorded in both spoken and written formats. The main purpose of this project is to ensure that these tragic stories are not allowed to fade into oblivion but are rather recorded accurately and impartially to leave firsthand sources for future generations. We also aim to bring this persecution to the attention of academics, media organizations, human rights associations, prominent community leaders, and government representatives at the international level.

"Escape from Turkey" is the product of a long-term endeavor. Each of our works is a compilation of real-life stories encountered by victims whose true names and event details have not been revealed for the safety of their families in Turkey. We would like to thank everyone who made tireless and valuable contributions to this work. We wish that Turkey will soon transform into a democratic society in which fundamental values like universal human rights and the rule of law are duly observed.

We sincerely thank Davut D. and Yakup Y. for sharing their stories with us. We would also like to thank our author Zeynep Kayadelen, editor Eyyup Esen, illustrators Yolgezer, A.O., A. B, and everyone else who contributed to this project.

THE
FORSAKEN
TREASURE

As told by Davut D.

FOREWORD

The following story is based on real events and people. The distinguished scientist, Professor Davut, who is the main character of the story, has not authorized us to share his real name, identity and some other personal information for safety concerns.

This story is just one of the thousands of stories of persecution. The human being has sought the purpose of his existence since he came to earth. When he used his greed and ambition as a compass, he tried to build palaces for himself at the expense of other people's tears. But each time, sooner or later, he would end up losing it all. This is how it has been and will continue to be.

The only thing man can take away from this world is love and compassion. The servants of God who bring love and

compassion with them will find God's Mercy there.

That's why even if others have made us suffer,

we will never give up love and compassion.

Zeynep Kayadelen

Lies can be very redundant, tempting, and deceptive;

but it is the Truth which is immortal...

THE FORSAKEN TREASURE

RISKING DEATH

I wondered if this was the end. All I could see was the dark and deep cemetery that I was about to ride on, the waters of the Maritsa River. Bubbling around in my head, I had only one idea: to be able to get out of my beloved country.

I felt like I was in a baby's crib as the river moved us along. Me, my brother-in-law, my cousin, and the young family with three kids. The youngest member of the family was a baby, and she was crying. The smuggler who accompanied us swore and said: "Shut her up; we will be caught." He was an aggressive type, swearing on every occasion. The possibility of getting caught before we could cross the river made me shudder. I whispered to my brother-in-law: "If we get caught, I'm going to jump into the water and swim." He said anxiously: "The water is not as it looks like; there's current and mud, you can get drowned, God forbid." In the middle of the dark night, I stared at the dark and cold waters of the Maritsa River and thought: "Am I not dead already, anyhow?" Being slandered and persecuted in a place where there was no rule of law, I was being suffocated and I had already experienced death in a sense. Everything we owned, including our destiny, was in the power of others' tongues. That was the kind of life that we were living, if it could be called living. I had to take risks to achieve freedom. The baby felt the anxiety that surrounded all of us and began to cry even louder. Her mother pressed the baby's head against her chest to make her stop crying. We all held our breaths.

So, how did things come to this? Why did I risk death? Let me tell you about it from the beginning. When I finished veterinary school in my hometown twelve years ago, I had a dream: To go abroad to make a career and then return to my country to serve my people. Meanwhile, I got married and went together with my wife to Germany. I was so eager to learn German and at the end of the first year, my German was sufficient to start working as a surgical assistant in a clinic. In the meantime, I was looking for career opportunities, I was determined to be an academician. I applied to a Ph.D. program at the University of Giessen and thank God, I was accepted. After four years, I got my Ph.D. degree. I was doing research on the causes of breast cancer and metabolic diseases, as well as on identifying molecular targets[1] to find drugs to cure these diseases. When I had laid the groundwork

---

1   A molecular target (or drug target) refers to the key molecules in the body (such as carbohydrates, proteins, and nucleic acids) that are involved in certain metabolic pathways leading to certain diseases.

for further scientific studies, I continued to work for three more months and then decided to return back to Turkey. Some people around me regarded my decision as being foolish. After all, I had a good job in a prosperous country where so many people wanted to live and the opportunities in Turkey were limited. But despite what the others said, in 2009, I returned to Turkey. I was determined to transmit my knowledge and experience to my country and to my people. I had learned in the Hizmet[2] movement to serve my people. Alas! I was soon to be brought to trial, on account of being affiliated with the same movement.

Shortly after I was assigned to the Pharmacology department at one of the universities in Turkey and became an associate professor a year later. It wasn't easy to work as a scientist in Turkey's conditions. There was neither financial nor motivational support. If you're not a famous singer or a soccer player, it's hard to draw attention. In fact, the lack of awareness of research and innovations in universities and the commonly used rote learning methods bothered me. The routine of "lecturing students-going home-enjoying yourself" was not precisely my way of teaching.

I was also advising my children to live unselfishly to help other people around. If you don't put your hands under the stone to change what you're complaining about, you are just a part of the

---

2   Hizmet (Service) Movement is a worldwide transnational civil society initiative that advocates for the ideals of human rights, equal opportunity, democracy, non-violence and the emphatic acceptance of religious and cultural diversity. For more information: www.afsv.org

problem. I was going to do my best, despite the limited research funding. Also, right after I had returned to Turkey, I had done six months of military service even though I did not have to. I had thought that I should have done it. Fulfilling all my responsibilities as a citizen of my country was like a worship service for me. The mere sight of our flag was enough to bring tears to my eyes.

Like I mentioned, the opportunities and funds were limited, but my efforts were bearing fruit. I was working twelve hours a day and sometimes even on weekends. At my university and several other scientific platforms, I received six awards in different categories such as successful scientist, patent, and best research project. I made a lot of progress in my research. The use of therapy 'X' in the rapid recovery of bone fractures were showing promising results. Substance 'X' was abundantly available in Turkey and had miraculous effects. To use it as a medicine would bring incredible benefits and advantages to the country. We had a TUBITAK[3] project. We were soon going to announce this new medical treatment. I was very excited and happy. I was just counting down the days to dedicate my invention's patent to my beloved country.

Ironically, my country had a gift for me, too. Unfortunately, some people were going to open Pandora's box on the night of July 15, 2016. Terrible days were waiting for me, nothing would have been the same since that Friday night. The scientist who made significant breakthrough in medical research, the esteemed Professor Davut, Ph.D. would be labeled as a terrorist and traitor overnight, at the request of some people. It was almost like a dark magic spell was placed on the country by an evil witch, good was to be called evil and evil was to be called good by the next morning.

PANDORA'S BOX

That day, I was with my family at home, it was quite an ordinary day. But after my sister's text message that evening, nothing was ever the same again. She told us to turn on the TV. I did it right away. TV channels were mentioning a military coup that had begun a few hours ago. Yes, military coup! That primitive fight for power, seen in the third world countries... Like millions of people, I was shocked. Four years have passed since then and I still have not gotten over with it. I slumped down onto sofa with the remote in my hand. My wife and I were staring at each other. Anxiety and sadness had fallen upon us like a nightmare. My concern was primarily for my country. These ridiculous coups were repeating themselves every 10-15 years and our country was getting weaker, both economically and socially. Because of those coups, our nation couldn't develop and our country couldn't get to the place that it deserved to be in the world. I was so upset; I wouldn't be more upset if they had told me that my house was on fire. However, in the aftermath of what happened, I should have felt sorry for myself. I didn't know then.

On TV channels, they were claiming that Hizmet movement volunteers were the ones who attempted this bloody act that could wage a civil war. The head of the government had already identified the culprits of the ongoing coup and was promising to take revenge. I said: "This is not right, Hizmet movement volunteers have nothing to do with guns. Obviously, there's a misunderstanding and the truth will come out soon." But that is not what happened. In the morning, in spite of the rising sun, a thick darkness was glooming over my country. Alas! When I utter these words, *"my country"*, my lips are trembling. I am so resentful, offended, and hurt.

It was a very long night for us. We could neither sleep nor be occupied with anything else. It was as if all hell broke loose, the streets were buzzing with the sounds of prayers coming from every mosque in the neighborhood. To be honest, I was terrified, especially for my country. I was a man who believed that no one could gain anything in a bloody gunfight. Whoever was leading this was pushing the country into deep chaos. I prayed all night until morning.

That night I went out to the streets following the president's call on TV to rise up against the coup, to demonstrate my disapproval. Now in grief, I'm laughing at my foolishness. I assume the real culprits laughed at us as well, on that night. Why? Because they had already framed people like me as culprits of the coup, although we had learned about it only on TV. It happens to be that they had even planned a long time ago, which people to arrest on that very night. They had already decided who the culprits were and all that was left was to stage a conspiracy to create the element of crime.

That night, I had thought about so many things. I wondered what my college professors in Germany were going to think of us.

What could one think about a country that expended its own people so quickly like a self-biting snake? I am sure they were very sad. I was full of shame on behalf of my country.

Our hearts were in distress, and we were so confused. All night long, we called our family members and friends. Everyone was asking one another the same questions: "What is going on? What shall we do?" Some of us were optimistic and some were pessimistic, but none of us was able to predict what was going to happen next. What we had in common was that we were very sad. A friend of mine said: "They will not let us breathe anymore." I didn't agree with him at all. Okay, the government might have a grudge against the Hizmet movement, but there was law and justice in the country, after all. They weren't going to blame or punish us for a crime we didn't commit!

It was like doomsday on social media, too. There were those who were talking about arming and going down the streets, who were making war proclamations, insults, threats... According to what they were saying, they were the patriots, the heroes, the best. So then, who were those dark people pointing guns at people?

What doubled my grief was that the government officials were very confident that the Hizmet movement was responsible for the coup. How come they were so sure about the culprit's identity while things were still going on? I had a hunch that hard times were waiting for Hizmet movement volunteers. That was what I thought for them, but not for myself. And I still can't forgive myself for not foreseeing what was going to happen to me.

Those who had framed Hizmet movement for this act, which is in total contrast to the spirit of the Hizmet movement, could have also claimed in the near future that I murdered someone. I wish I would have left the country that night instead of being so foolish to hope that the fire surrounding me would be extinguished and everything would be just fine. But then again, I am a man who believes in fate. Thus, even when they put me in prison later, I never said: "I wish I hadn't come back to Turkey, in the first place." although it came to my mind. What I went through was because of my good intention and I wouldn't regret it. You offer a rose to someone with all your good feelings, but that person thinks ill of your intentions and perceives that rose as a weapon and punches you. Well, other peoples' evil hearts can't be your fault. The day that you stop offering roses, that you give up spreading goodness, and that you regret for your past good actions... yes, that would be the day when you would be defeated by evil.

It's been four years and that coup is still like a black box to me, I still don't know who did what on that night and why. I genuinely believe that the truth will come out sooner or later. Eventually, the perpetrators of that evil plan that spilled blood over that night will be soaked with sweat under the sun of truth. And they will be held accountable. I will demand answers, too. I will hold them responsible for my dreams they have shattered and for every second of my life that I have suffered because of their slanders.

HIDDEN CAMERA PRANK

I had not slept at all on that night, but I still wished all that I saw was just a dream. Alas! It wasn't. The next day, I got an e-mail calling all the faculty and staff to the university that I was working for. Meanwhile, I was still keeping my optimism. Yes, obviously some people got armed and attempted a plot against democracy, but luckily, they were intercepted. I was thinking, those people would be caught and brought to justice, so eventually the country would go back into its routine. But when I arrived at the university, I realized it wasn't going to be that easy. Everyone was acting weird; staring at each other in anger and with fear. The atmosphere was so tense. The eyes, which were smiling at me until two days ago, were now staring at me, skeptical and anxiously. Everyone around knew that I was close to the Hizmet movement. I guess they assumed that I was supporting the coup as well. It seemed like they had already accepted the baseless accusations made by the government that night.

Supposedly, some Hizmet movement volunteers got armed and murdered many people to topple the government and to occupy the country, but they had failed to do so. This was a ridiculous claim, absolutely baseless from both a rational and legal standpoint, yet so many people in the society had accepted it. Think about it, why would you occupy the country you already live in? Or why would you want to topple the government when you don't even have a political party? Besides, even if several people in the Hizmet movement had participated in actions like these, why would I be held accountable for their actions, when I was at home playing with my children?

On August 12, 2016, I was suspended from my job at university where everyone had already abandoned me as if I were stricken by a plague. This was the date when I had received a written notification, but the decision on my suspension was made on July 17, 2016. I didn't expect it, even though I had seen so many radical people on the streets who were screaming and ready to lynch Hizmet movement volunteers. Actually, I didn't have any kind of duty in any kind of association. I was just reading Fethullah Gulen's[4] books and trying to establish my prayers and do my job in the best way possible as he was explaining in his books.

A lot of my friends had been suspended during this period. Our neighbors, relatives, and friends were changing their direction when they saw us walking around. After the night of the coup, I had been through so many absurd things that I could not stop asking: "Is this really happening?" You know, like the hidden camera pranks when the guy gets shocked and then you say: "Wave to the camera." We were shocked, but no one came and said: "It's a prank, wave to the camera."

---

4   Fethullah Gulen is a Turkish Muslim scholar, thinker, author, poet, opinion leader and educational activist who supports interfaith and intercultural dialogue, science, democracy and spirituality. He opposes violence and turning religion into a political ideology. For more information: https://fgulen.com/en

Everyone considers others as themselves. I could not know what evil spirits could do. Even though I was smart enough to make a scientific breakthrough, I was still naively hoping that things would get better. I was suspended, but I was going to take my grievance to court! Typically, the university would have opened an investigation after an employee was suspended. Papers would be delivered to me, questions would be asked, and I would defend myself. I was waiting for the paperwork at home. But I was waiting in vain. I didn't get anything but bills in my mailbox.

I reached out to the committee members at my university and asked: "I haven't received yet the investigation documents about me. I will prepare my defense accordingly. When would they come?" The answer from a committee member was very interesting: "There is no need to send an investigation document for some cases." Being shuddered, I thought that this sentence could mean one of two things: Either "We know you are innocent, so there's no need for a defense" or "We are certain that you are guilty and the verdict is already given." My inner voice was telling me it was the second. Do you know why? Because the decision of the YOK[5] to suspend me was dated July 17, 2016. So, just two days after the July 15th coup, they had "proven" (!) that I was involved in the armed organization that attempted the coup and then suspended me, without any evidence whatsoever. According to the Turkish government, FETO[6], an "armed terrorist organization" was now

---

5   Council of Higher Education in Turkey.
6   A so-called terrorist organization, referred as such only by the Erdogan Government in

the new name of the Hizmet movement. The government had come up with this name. And how much sense does it make to believe that it took just a few hours to the government to make serious accusations against tens of thousands of people for being a member of a terrorist organization and having a role in the coup? Just think about it.

And that was not all. Just two days after the coup, eleven professors at my university were detained and handcuffed behind their backs with their heads bowed. Who gets such a treatment usually? If police chase an armed criminal and then catch him, that criminal is handcuffed and then taken into custody. But these people who were accused of being members of the Hizmet movement were ordinary citizens. That night, some of them were attending a wedding ceremony, some were at a soccer game, some doing this, some doing that. But they had nothing to do with the coup attempt whatsoever. Why were they exposed to this ill treatment based on nothing? I had mentioned previously that, since so many years ago, people who are close to the Hizmet movement were recorded by authorities illegally, name by name. July 15th offered them an opportunity to put their dark plans into practice, just like the way they once let it slip out of their mouths.

When medical scientists and respected professors were

Turkey, otherwise known as Gulen Movement or Hizmet (Service) Movement worldwide, a transnational civil society initiative that advocates for the ideals of human rights, equal opportunity, democracy, non-violence and the emphatic acceptance of religious and cultural diversity. For more information: www.afsv.org

handcuffed and being taken away, I was still thinking that nothing would happen to me. I couldn't be sure of anyone else, but I was sure of my own innocence. Or was I? Ironically, when I was later sentenced to prison, they made me doubt myself that perhaps I had committed a crime. It was a momentary hesitation. When I was behind bars, I was sure there was no such thing called 'FETO, an armed terrorist organization', there was nothing like the so-called 'parallel state structure.' I was not guilty, but there were some evil people in the world. They were so evil, it was even beyond my perception. So many conspiracies were going on around us, we had seen them only in movies until then.

UNFINISHED COFFEE

I was suffering from severe anxiety since the night of the coup attempt, the increasing stress was getting unbearable. My psychology was all disrupted due to the incomprehensible injustices done not only to me but also to so many innocent people. I was not able to sleep during nights. I was wandering so nervously inside the house with bloody red eyes, with suspicion that more calamities were soon to happen. I was deeply worried that my loved ones would get hurt and I wouldn't be able to do anything to help them. The daytime was no different than the nighttime for me, either. I had this constant feeling that as if I were alone in a forest full of wild and ferocious animals. For Friday prayers, instead of the mosque in the university campus, I was going to mosques far away where no one knew me. Many people knew me in the campus because of my academic reputation and now that had become a mark against me. People who knew me, were turning their heads in opposite directions and running away like I had a contagious disease. Treason is the worst accusation for a person, they had put this label on me overnight and said: "This is you, a traitor!" Some people were running away from me because they just hated me, some were just afraid of being seen with me. I was getting stoned and lynched, psychologically and socially, by attitudes and words. I was brutally tortured, emotionally, since the night of the coup. A hand was on my throat, choking me.

Evil people can exist in any society. However, there was another type of evil in this country, which was so devastating to observe: An ignorant majority who had not learned a single thing about the rule of law and justice. They considered lynching as doing justice. Think about it, someone just points his finger at you and everyone attacks you all of a sudden, with no hesitation. That was pretty much the picture. No one cared about the rule of law, about *the principle of individual criminal responsibility[7]*. It was sufficient for you to be labeled as a terrorist if you didn't openly declare that you hated Fethullah Gulen. On the way to prison, my inner voice was whispering: "Wake up professor, wake up! Welcome to the real world!"

As for going to jail... The police came to our house on yet another Friday. After Friday prayer around noon, I had called my father who was very worried about what was going on. I tried to comfort him, saying: "We're not guilty of anything, everything's going to be all right." although the daily news was filled up with the stories of thousands of people getting arrested every day; sadly, they were not guilty of anything, either.

I came home and I said to my wife: "Let's have a cup of coffee." My wife was a smart person and she was frequently saying no one could be charged with any crime without any evidence: "One cannot be labeled as a terrorist just because he was subscribed to a

---

7   Turkish Panel code, Article 20/1: Criminal responsibility is personal. No one shall be deemed culpable for the conduct of another.

newspaper years ago."[8] She was trying to cheer me up during those hard times. Under these circumstances, I considered myself lucky because some of my friends' wives had filed for divorce.

We were drinking coffee with my wife together. I couldn't know then that I wouldn't be able to drink another cup of coffee like this for a long time. There was a knock at the door before we finished our coffee. I opened the door and there were a bunch of cops in front of me. They said they had a search warrant. I responded: "OK, you may search, but what are you looking for?" They didn't say what they were looking for. I stepped aside and made way. The government's hatred was officially in my house. Though, most of these cops would later end up sharing my destiny. I guess only one of them kept his job later and he was the one who had treated me with prejudice and scolded me like I was guilty. In every government institution, people were easily labeled as terrorists and those with conscience couldn't survive anywhere.

---

8   Turkish Panel code, Article 7/1: No person shall be subject to a penalty or security measure for any act which did not constitute a criminal offence under the law in force at the time it was committed. No one shall be subject to a penalty or security measure for an act which does not constitute an offence according to the law which came into force after the commission of the offence. Where such a penalty or security measure has been imposed its enforcement and the legal consequences of such shall be automatically set aside.

All of the individuals who were trialed in "July 15 related" courts, were found guilty and sentenced accordingly, for the acts which did not constitute a criminal offence under the law in force at the time it was committed, or even at the time of those trials. Some of those so-called "criminal offenses" were being subscribed to the best-selling newspaper in Turkey, Zaman, which was in circulation since 1986; having an account in Bank Asya, which was one of the biggest banks in Turkey since 1996; and choosing the schools affiliated with Hizmet Movement for your children to attend.

At home, they found nothing as crime evidence but my daughter's book and a calendar. And the reason that they were considered to be evidence of crime is because they were published by a publishing house which was banned only a few weeks ago. Luckily, my eldest daughter wasn't home and she didn't see the cops searching the entire house, including even the pots in the kitchen. They were almost done and about to leave, but after a phone call, they said there was a detention warrant for me. My wife was crying silently. This was the beginning of the coming horrible days. The way that things unfolded since the coup was beyond my imagination. All I could think about was when would this madness end. I put a few clothes in a small bag, kissed my one-year-old daughter, and left my house accompanied by cops on August 26, 2016. Neighbors were at windows, watching the arrest of the 'dangerous terrorist.' Yes, the entire nation was just watching, while the lives of thousands of innocent people were being destroyed, while the TV networks were justifying the mass arrests and tortures and while even our children were being isolated and harassed in their schools.

OH, BOY! YOU'RE A SCIENTIST!

I knew more or less how much a person would hurt if you punched him. Well, now I was learning how much it would hurt if you lynched a man's honor and dignity and accused him of betraying his beloved homeland. It was unbearable. When I was being put in the police car, I was hurting so bad, my heart was breaking into thousands of pieces. They were destroying my soul.

They took me first to my office at the university. They searched there, too. I was walking down the hallways between the cops and people who once were following me around and calling me "Professor" were now staring at me suspiciously. Alas! Slander is indeed murder; I was dying slowly, I couldn't breathe, staggering as I walked. As if the coup on the night of July 15th had been done against me. Psychologically, they had broken me and sealed my mouth, only to label me as a terrorist, a traitor. I was no longer myself, but I was definitely not the person they said I was! It was like something was stuck in my throat and I was choking: "Why? Why all this torture? What have I done to deserve this?"

After leaving my office, I was taken for a doctor's check-up to a hospital, together with a group of other detainees like me. At the hospital, the doctors and other patients were so nervous and uncomfortable around us. It was as if we had a terrible infectious disease and what's more, that we had created this dreadful disease just for being evil. When they noticed us, they were stepping back, standing as far away as they could and swearing and cursing quietly.

Finally, we were brought to a gym which was arranged as a detention center. Because of the witch hunt, the standard police stations were full to the brim. There were 120 people at this place with windows covered with thick curtains, most of us knew each other. I was a little relieved to see familiar faces. They were all very successful academicians in their field. I thought the prosecutor would release such respected academicians in a few days. There was no reason to think otherwise. In fact, I even made plans for the upcoming Eid-ul Adha[9], while waiting. I would take my family to our hometown to visit our relatives. I still had not realized that I was pretty much a sheep to be slaughtered.

The detention period, which was supposed to only be for a few days, lasted a week. But to me, it felt like years. I felt like being chained in a dark cave for years, with no sense of time. We were sleeping on sports mats on the floor, using our jackets as pillows. Our breakfast was three olives, a piece of bread, and a small pack of jam. A weird soup for lunch and porridge pasta for dinner. I was trying to eat in order to survive.

They had taken my watch; hence I had lost the sense of time. No book to read, no pen or paper to write something. We paced back

---

9   An Islamic holiday celebrated worldwide each year. It honors the willingness of Ibrahim (Abraham) to sacrifice his son as an act of obedience to God's command. Before Ibrahim could sacrifice his son, however, God provided a lamb to sacrifice instead.

and forth, prayed, and tried to make sense of what was happening to us. There were cameras everywhere. What caught my attention was that there were 120 of us, but only two guards. Imagine two cops among 120 "terrorists," they were even sleeping among us every now and then. It's beyond ludicrous, isn't it? Obviously, even the police were aware that we were harmless. So, what was this all about?

It was incredible to see that the society had been poisoned against us. The government had shown us to the masses of the people as the root of all the problems. One of the guards was a young police officer from the city Adana, he was looking at us with hatred, scolding and swearing at us. As we were disconnected from the outside world, we were either asking about the time or requesting an attorney, but he just kept saying that he hated us and talked about his police friends who died in Ankara on the night of the coup. I was trying to explain to him that we had nothing to do with the coup and sometimes he seemed to understand a little bit, but then he would go back to his rude manners. The day I got out of custody, that cop was on duty again. We were going to the court. They were calling us in turns. As I walked past him, he stood up and said silently: "Professor, I searched your story on the internet, you are a real scientist; may God help you, I hope you get out of this."

WE DON'T LIKE YOU,

THEREFORE YOU ARE GUILTY!

We were held longer in custody than what was allowed by law. The procedure was even more torturous than what was done to criminals. We were taken to courthouse early in the morning, and after being held from morning till late afternoon, we were finally called by name into the court hall. I thought this mockery would end there and I would go home.

When I confronted the prosecutor, who appeared to have some kind of psychological problems and who was frequently making strange hand gestures, he said: "There's a ByLock[10] app on your phone." When I objected, he scolded me and ordered me to sit, saying, "Would you know better than us?" I had a lawyer that my parents hired with great difficulties. During that time period, no lawyer wanted to defend someone attributed to the Hizmet movement. To my shock, my lawyer turned to me and said, "Look professor, you have kids. Give us the names of three Hizmet members and go home as a free man." The lawyer's words broke me yet again. "Didn't you come here to defend me?" I responded: "Besides, I don't know anyone who's a member of a terrorist organization. I can't give you any names." The prosecutor got more frustrated hearing what I said. He yelled in anger, "Get out! I'm sending you to the court with the request for an arrest." he said. This weird guy that I didn't know seemed to have a personal grudge against me. I realized the reason afterward: The prosecutors and judges who treated us the worst were getting promoted by the government and assigned to better positions.

The trial phase wasn't how I expected it, either. I thought it was going to be like the courts in the movies. We would go into the courtroom, the judge would sit in front, we would sit behind a bench, my lawyer would be on my right. We were expecting an opportunity in which we could defend ourselves. That was not how it happened. We waited in the hallway and were called to the bailiff's room one by one. Two people were sitting there. One of them said my name, last name, and my home address. When I heard my address, I was shocked for a moment; it was obvious that everything was pretty much staged a long time ago. Because the address they told me belonged to the apartment we lived in three years ago. Imagine that even I had forgotten my old address, but they had recorded it. Why was an ordinary citizen under such surveillance? If I had committed a crime, why didn't they arrest me then? If there was no crime, why did they keep record of my name and address? I guess those who didn't like the Hizmet movement's activities never stayed idle. The judge claimed I was using the ByLock app on my cellphone. I emphasized: "I didn't download ByLock." He scolded me: "If it was not you, who did it? Me?" and added: "Do you have anything to say?" I said: "Even if I downloaded ByLock, it wouldn't be a criminal act. I am innocent." My lawyer asked for my acquittal and they took me out of the room. There were twelve people in the hallway with me.

When the individual interrogations were over, they brought us all back in. We stood in two rows in front of the judge. "I'm arresting all of you." he said without making eye contact, as if he was saying something so trivial. It was all over. I was out of breath. I loosened my tie, I felt like no oxygen was getting to my lungs. Puzzled, I looked at the friend next to me who was screaming: "I didn't commit a crime; you can't do this!" I was frozen. They pushed us out of the hall. I didn't know who did the July 15th coup, but I knew those who were giving me fatal blows ever since. It was a crowd which was pretty much saying, "We don't like you and never did!" and they were striking harder and more deadly. At the request of some people I had never met, my life was being dragged to an unsustainable point. My brain was numbed and I wished someone to stop this hidden camera prank. No one was saying stop. The government was trying to create savage terrorists out of innocent people, saying, "Yes, you are a terrorist! I insist on this!" Shouldn't it usually be the opposite? Shouldn't the government try to rehabilitate the culprit? My consciousness was in a state of shock, flickering in panic. I couldn't understand anymore what was going on. I took deep breaths, took refuge in God, and decided to stop looking for an explanation. I had to survive for my baby daughter who was not even able to walk yet.

We were arrested now; the bailiff gave us our papers and cops armed with rifles immediately surrounded and handcuffed us. When the arrest order was given, we became confirmed terrorists. Before we went to prison, they took us back to hospital for another medical checkup. It was a routine procedure. Actually, regardless of whether they were a doctor or a cop, most people wished we were dead and they didn't even mind to say that. I had a so-called health checkup that night among the doctors and patients who were all insulting me with their looks. The doctor pretty much pretended to examine me and then scribbled something on paper, with a sour look on his face. They were using every opportunity to crush us and turn us into a grain of dust.

I was planning to spend the Eid-ul Adha with my family in Erzurum. Instead, I was taken to an H-type prison in the same city. On the way to prison, I thought and got worried about the prison conditions. With whom would I be staying in prison? I really didn't want to be in the same ward with the real criminals who had hurt someone. Fortunately, this didn't happen. Their policy was placing members of the same organization in the same ward. It was written on the court records that I was a member of the so called FETO[11] organization allegedly founded by Hizmet movement volunteers. Well, at least I'd be among decent people in the ward.

We arrived at prison around 2:00 a.m. While we were passing the hallways and iron doors, guards were pushing us as they wished.

---

11   See footnote 6 on page 28

In one of the hallways with dirty walls, we stood in front of a ward under dim light. The people inside woke up because of the noise that the iron door made. When I saw a clean-faced, middle-aged prisoner who greeted me, I pulled myself together. His face was so bright, I felt at peace. "Welcome, Brother," the prisoner said with a warm smile. I was moved by his effort to host me when he was in the same situation. I said to myself, "God, these people can't have done anything bad and I didn't do anything bad." That kind man was trying to comfort me. "Don't worry, Brother, we'll help you with everything." he said. I owe him a debt of gratitude for what he did.

BURIED ALIVE

I was a prisoner now. The iron door closed on us loudly. I sat on my bed. I thought about what was going on. That night, I felt like waking up from a deep sleep that I had been living in. I realized that my life that I was seeing through rose-colored glasses was nothing but a glass ball in the hands of some monsters. Whenever they wanted, they could easily smash it into pieces. I pretty much hit rock bottom. They had taken my everything away from me. They had seized all our assets, but the most important thing was that they had stolen my job and my dreams. They were crushing the honor of humanity under their feet and they were doing it with joy and laughter. I looked at the semi-dark room under the dim light of the hallway. I felt like buried alive in a grave. Without the trust in God and His divine justice, a man couldn't stand this. For someone who did not believe in the Hereafter, the destruction of his world meant the end of everything. However, I believed in God and the justice of the Hereafter, where the people who had done this to me would be held accountable. On that day, I would spit in the faces of those cruel and slanderous people and it would be payback time. This was what made me stand tall between those four walls where I was buried alive.

I found out that if you were patient enough, there was nothing that you couldn't get used to. By the end of the first week, I was already getting the hang of being in prison. Early in the mornings I was getting up for prayer and then I was mostly reading books until midnight, books related to my profession and otherwise. We were purchasing some of the books from outside; some of them we borrowed from the prison library; and sometimes we traded them among us. But the prison guards were creating trouble even with the books. They had nonsensical restrictions about many things, including books.

Illustrated by Yolgezer

Everyone in the ward was given a blanket, a mattress, and a chair. My coat was still serving as a pillow because they had not given one. We were fourteen people staying in a 50-square-meter ward which was normally designed for three people. At 8:00 a.m., the guards were coming to count us, opening the door to the small courtyard outside and half an hour later, breakfast was distributed. The amount of jam, bread, and olives they were giving was sufficient only for a few people and we were fourteen. Fortunately, we were able to buy breakfast from the prison canteen. Those who could afford it were sharing what they bought with people who didn't have any money. Some of them were so kind, they were buying things like disposable razors or snacks in boxes and putting them on a desk with a sign attached next to them: "Free." The kindness and helpfulness of these people was fetching tears from my eyes. These people were accused of being a member of an armed terrorist organization! Everyone was taking care of each other. Some of our friends were rejected by their families and didn't receive any financial or emotional support; we were all watching over them. Even though I still couldn't understand why I was in prison and why I had been put through all this, there were so many things to thank God for. I was with good friends, friends who would help you find your way and increase the goodness in your heart like a candlelight that illuminates your path. As the saying goes: "You become like the people you spend the most time with. Birds of a feather flock together."

One night they brought in a young college student, who was

19 or 20 years old. When he walked into the ward, we stood up and welcomed him. The young man told the guards who brought him: "I am sorry, I've bothered you at this nighttime." Hearing that, we couldn't help laughing. We knew that the people of the Hizmet movement had a gentle character, but this was the first time we had witnessed such an extreme example. Even the guard was surprised to hear that, he didn't know what to say, he just walked away.

One day during breakfast, I saw scratches on that student's arms. I got so sad, thinking that they perhaps had tortured him. He said: "No Brother, I was not tortured. I was in the country town to help my family in harvesting. These scratches are due to that. They arrested me while I was working in the field."

He was such a gentle young man. I had noticed that during the nights, he was just leaning on the wall and sleeping like that. I asked him why he was not sleeping in his bed. We all were shocked upon hearing his answer: "How could I extent my legs and sleep like that while I am among such precious people like you, Professor?" Imagine, they had accused such a gentle person of being a terrorist.

What is more, just to make room for people like him in the crowded prisons, the government had released thousands of real criminals who had murdered people, raped, and robbed. Who could bear all this injustice? But I had to survive. The prophet Joseph was slandered, too; and he had managed to turn the dark prison into an advantage. They had taken everything I had, but I was content. I was thankful because I wasn't on the side of the people who persecuted us. I was hurt, but thank God I was not like them, I was not hurting anyone.

DADDY! PLEASE TURN THE CAMERA ON!

One day we were in the courtyard again. The yards of three different wards were separated by a wall. There were tiny holes in the wall so you could talk to people at the other side. In the adjacent ward, there were prisoners of Kurdish origin, convicted for being a member of a different terrorist organization. We heard them thumping on the wall several times. Apparently, they wanted to talk to us. Of course, all my friends were scared at first because this was the first time we had been in an environment like this; we didn't know who was who, there were real criminals in other wards. They kept thumping on the wall. At last, I plucked up some courage to talk to them. The man behind the wall spoke broken Turkish; nevertheless, he was able to explain the ongoing events with sociological phrases. The first thing he asked me was: "Did you guys attempt the July 15th coup?" I told him that we had absolutely nothing to do with it. He kept silent. Then I asked him: "Since it was not us, who do you think did it?" He said that that the government had staged this coup together with some other groups. We were all shocked by his answer because we were not expecting an analysis like this from them. So, this was it? Pretty much everyone knew about the truth behind the coup.

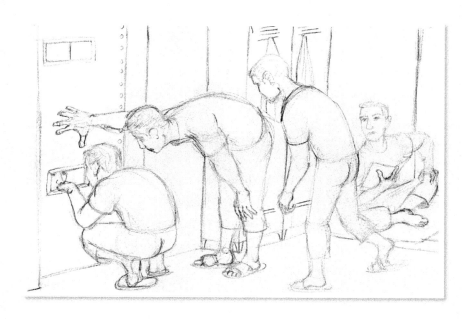

Illustrated by Yolgezer

The days were passing between four walls. Some of the guards were just doing their job, but some of them were insulting us on every occasion. Sometimes they were even threatening us. To some extent, they were doing it to protect themselves. This "new terrorist organization" was created as a bogeyman and everyone was supposed to stone this bogeyman. The guards knew they would end up sharing our destiny if they didn't stone us every now and then. Members of the judiciary, guards, prisoners… the majority was not aware of the ominous vicious circle they were in. Pretty much, everyone was gloomy and distressed. The tension in the entire society was so thick since the night of the coup. It was as if an invisible hand had taken away the joy from the hearts and the smile from the faces.

Even though we doubted the existence of the rule of law, we didn't give up on the legal struggle. I had written a lot of petitions to appeal, none of them were taken into consideration. The other prisoners thought I'd stay inside for a long time because it was a judge in a court who had ordered for my arrest. Some of my ward mates were in prison for a few years and they had not been to the court, not even once. People were being punished for the crimes they had not committed. Since we weren't the perpetrators of the coup, the real plotters of the coup were out there. What direction were we headed in? Quo Vadis? What was the direction of all these events? As Nasreddin Hodja[12] said: "They had leashed the stones and unleashed the dogs." During my daily prayers, I was crying for my country.

One of the most challenging things in prison was that I had no visitors. I didn't have the excitement and joy that everyone else experienced on the days of family visits. After I was imprisoned, my wife and I had decided together that they should return to Germany, where my wife's parents were living. I didn't want my wife and children to live in the gloomy atmosphere of Turkey.

Illustrated by Yolgezer

We were allowed 10-minute phone conversation every two weeks. Whenever I was on the phone with my nine-year-old daughter, she was insisting on a video call. Every single time she was begging me, "Dad, turn on the camera." I was making up different excuses and saying I couldn't turn on the camera. My wife had not told my daughter that I was in prison. She thought that I was on a business trip. Later I found out that my daughter was becoming introverted day by day. She wasn't talking to anyone. My wife eventually consulted a psychologist about my daughter's condition. The psychologist advised to tell her the truth about my situation. When my wife told her that I was unfairly arrested and that I was in jail, my daughter got so happy. It turns out that my dear daughter had thought we were getting divorced and hiding this from her! She just couldn't accept me leaving them. On our first phone call after learning the truth, she said that she loved me very much and believed that I was innocent. I told her we'd meet soon and to take good care of her sister. Would we really meet soon? We were all lost in a sea of uncertainty, desperately looking for a direction. How could we prove our innocence? How could we get out of this place where we were thrown? Uncertainty was the only sure thing about our future. I could understand my friends in the ward who were punching the walls. We were all advising each other to be patient. Our only weapon and consolation was patience and prayer.

6 YEARS AND 3 MONTHS

While counting the days and months, my one-and-a-half-year imprisonment ended with a new court decision. The end was as tragicomic as the beginning. This time the judge was a female wearing a headscarf. It was like I was among bullies in a neighborhood cafe, not in a courtroom. While I was making my plea, the judge and the prosecutor were talking to each other about what to eat for lunch. Imagine, your life is at stake and they are chatting and laughing, "Who's going to pay for lunch this time? How about we get gyro or kebab?" This judge, too, just pretended to listen to my defense, like the previous judge who had arrested me. And then she read a pre-made decision. On February 20, 2018, I was convicted with a six-year and three-month sentence for being a member of a terrorist organization. The decision would go to the Court of Cassation. Meanwhile, I would be released from the prison. If and when the Court of Cassation would approve the verdict, I would be imprisoned again. Of course, I was banned from traveling abroad, too.

While staying in prison, I thought that I was going to die of grief. I would never have believed it if someone had told me I'd be sad to leave prison. I had met many precious people there from whom I learned a great deal. It was probably the worst but the most special time period in my life. Like the splitting and then sprouting of a seed in the soil, I cracked and crushed due to suffering in that dark cell and new feelings sprouted in my heart each day. I became a whole different person. My faith was consolidated and I was absolutely sure of what I had to do in life. I realized how short and precious life is. I had to leave a pleasant memory under this eternal dome, as the poet Baki[13] had said.

When it was time to be released, I put my belongings into a trash bag. We cried as I hugged each of my ward mates who were victims of the same injustice and similar slanders. I left some of my belongings as a present. During these 18 months in prison, I had found everlasting brothers. I was embarrassed, like it was my fault to leave them behind. A part of me was staying with them and only when they were released, I would be totally free.

When I walked out of the prison door, everything was different. Even the air I breathed felt different. In addition to the absence of my wife and children, everyone, including most of my closest relatives, had turned away from me. The atmosphere of fear on the streets was so dense you could easily feel it. When the topic would turn to certain issues, the voices were lowered and everyone was looking around with fear. Some of the people I knew were telling me how sorry they were for me and how they thought that I had been subjected to ill treatment. I wanted to yell at them, "You should feel sorry for yourself!" I wished to tell them: "Can you be sure that

---

13 A Turkish poet who lived in the 16th century.

the hand which strangled an innocent person today won't knock on your door tomorrow?" I was expecting them to question the new order in the country; the order of oppressing, intimidating, and silencing the public. It was weird, everyone was scared to death, but they would still not say: "Things shouldn't have been like that." The majority was in the daily rush of making a living, paying attention to TV shows or soccer games. They were not interested in what had happened to us, not at all.

I was isolated. Even my closest friends did not want to call me on the phone. If we were going to meet, we picked places where there was no one else around and usually after midnight. Even those ones with different world views and whom I had always known to be so brave, had the same fear in their eyes: the fear of being seen with me in public. They were afraid of being subject of an investigation.

I said to myself, "It's better to die bravely than to live in fear." And I decided to leave the country, by any means necessary. By the way, even if you didn't leave, you would be doomed to starvation: no jobs around and no one to hire you. The government had declared you an enemy. I am not exaggerating when I say that if someone literally lynched you because you are a member of the Hizmet movement, that person would be rewarded instead of being punished. My relatives and friends were making excuses to stay away from me. My academic career, my research, my dreams were all halted. The research project I was working on didn't go any further because no one wanted to appear in the same frame with me as I was a "traitor." Here is the metaphor that I use to describe the halt of my research: I unearthed a treasure and I was running with a thrill to share it with my nation; but someone tripped me on the way and I fell down, the treasure got mixed back with the earth and lost. The chaotic atmosphere in the country was destroying every beautiful thing.

I was out of prison, so you would think that I was free. As the days passed, I was realizing that I was only transferred from a closed prison to an open prison. My hands were tied. I didn't feel safe. I was getting anxious when I saw a cop on the street or when the doorbell rang. If they would tell me, "Well, we pretty much decided that your sentence is life imprisonment." there was absolutely nothing I could do about it. I couldn't take this constant pressure anymore. I was in desperate need of feeling safe again and that need was not less than the need for a job.

Illustrated by A.B.

DARK, DEEP WATERS

My brother-in-law and my cousin were sympathized with the Hizmet movement, too. We gathered together and discussed what we should do. We agreed that we just couldn't continue to live in this country, under these circumstances. We started looking for ways to go abroad. We couldn't legally leave the country because we were banned from traveling abroad. So, what could we do? We decided to flee to Greece by crossing the Maritsa River, which was on the border of Greece and Turkey. We didn't talk about this to anyone except a few very close people. Turkey had become Nazi Germany. Who could we trust when people were snitching even on their closest relatives? A distraint order was issued for my car, but I had managed to cancel it and then sold the car. The money I received was my only financial resource. I used some of the money to pay the smugglers. We learned that there was such a business around Maritsa River, which was a popular transit way for many migrants and refugees.

The day had arrived on which I would escape from my country. Do you know how a person feels when he is forced to flee from his country that he loved so much? On the roads you pass, on the hills you look at for the last time, you leave a part of you; and you slowly vanish. At every step you take, you dig a grave and bury your dreams and joy of life. Leaving my homeland without knowing when I would see it again was very painful. It was very difficult for me to be a whole person again. They had ripped me apart, broken me into pieces.

We set out on the road. We passed through Istanbul, then Tekirdag and finally arrived at the border. We did not trust the smugglers either, but as the saying goes, a drowning man clutches at any straw. All day long, we spent time in Edirne. In the evening we met with others at a place close to the river. We were to cross the river together with a couple. They had three children, the youngest was a six-month-old baby girl. Her mother had given her a sedative so that she wouldn't cry and get us caught. The other kids were aware that they had to be quiet. We all piled into a car and drove for some time, then we started walking. We walked through swamps, dense bushes, and a pond. While I was in prison, I had pretty much learned to accept things as they presented themselves. But this was just too harsh. I burst into tears while walking away from my homeland at each step. "I don't deserve this!" screamed the little boy inside me. I wanted to shout out that our own government, our own people shouldn't have expended us so quickly; this shouldn't have happened at all. I had a lump in my throat and tears in my eyes. There was another voice inside me, whispering: "Do not grieve! So many others have been mistreated, as well. These lands, these rivers have witnessed so much cruelty." My mind was trying to comfort me, but my heart was broken. It was dark; no one saw me crying. My Lord saw it. My grief was rising up to the heavens.

After a long walk, we reached the boat that would carry us across the river. When we arrived on the shores of the Maritsa River, we hid in the bushes. There were so many giant mosquitoes around that place, and they bit us all over. It was then that the baby who was sleeping under the effect of the sedative woke up and started crying. While her mother was trying to quiet the baby, the smuggler was swearing: "Shut her up." We were praying silently for the baby to calm down. We waited there until dark, and the baby kept silent.

And this is the part I mentioned at the beginning of my story, the boat was moving through the dark waters of the Maritsa River. It was like we were in a horror movie. The older children, full of fear, snuggled with each other and kept silent. For the rest of my life, I will not forget the fear in those kids' eyes... The baby woke up and started crying again, maybe because of the mosquito bites. Her mother was trying to calm her down. The seconds felt like minutes, squeezing us. I was determined to jump into the water if the soldiers on patrol noticed us. I wanted to leave the country so bad, by any means necessary. Fortunately, without any problem, we arrived on the shore of the Greek side. It was April 28, 2018. A few steps more and we would be out of Turkey.

If it is your loved one who wrongs you,
you remain wounded even if you survive.

OH, FREEDOM!

It was rough to get out of the river. There was no safe spot around to reach the very steep shore. And we had to get off the boat before the bush thorns punctured it. We started climbing a hillside covered with bushes to get to the shore. Our hands and faces were torn and we got mud all over us. That stage was over, too, thank God. We were not in Turkey anymore, it was Greece. We kept walking, never stopped. After walking away from the shore, we changed our soaking wet clothes in the woods. It was pitch black. Half an hour later, the mother of the baby realized that during the rush, she had left the bag with the baby's belongings in the woods. I accompanied the baby's father all the way back to find the bag. We were worried. The darkness was to our advantage and disadvantage at the same time. We couldn't see where we were going. The possibility of getting caught was another cause of anxiety. Finally, we found the bag and then came back. We kept walking together with the others. We were all so jumpy as if a hand would grab us all of a sudden and drag us all the way back. We had to go through this tunnel of darkness to reach the light. This was not the time to stop. We had to move forward as far as we could. We walked for three more hours and reached a village. Easier said than done. We had crossed the border illegally and we did not know what to expect. We were a little relieved, though. At least we were in a land where there was law and justice.

The adults were doing okay, but the kids weren't so good. They were tired and cold. We were all so thirsty. We found the church of the village and drank water from the fountain in the yard and established our night prayers. It was so cold; we lit a fire using the sticks and twigs around to warm up the kids. I was shivering due to fatigue and stress. We lay down on the benches of the church outside, but it was freezing cold, so we decided to walk again to warm up. After another four-hour walk I was exhausted, but I felt much better mentally. I was feeling as if was really out of prison now. I had left that unsafe place in which people were thinking that it was their patriotic duty to torture me. But I was not feeling happy. If it is your loved one who wrongs you, you remain wounded even if you survive. My soul was wounded, my heart was broken.

Sun had risen while we were walking down the road. We were covered in mud, looking so miserable when a police car approached us. They stopped us and asked: "Are you coming from Turkey?" We replied, "Yes." Then they said: "Do not worry; we know about what is going on there." It had been such a long time that I had not seen any kind of understanding from anyone, so upon hearing their comforting words, my eyes filled with tears. They told us that they were going to host us for a few days. We gave our passports and they took us to the police station.

There were people from other countries who stayed with us in custody. So many people from all colors who had left their homelands. They were so anxious, full of fear, having lost their everything recently. I got very upset about them, too. The way the police treated us was different from how they treated them. I don't know whether it was because we had prestigious professions or because they knew it very well that we were being mistreated in our country. They were very kind to us. I still pray for the Greek police and Greek people because of their hospitality to us.

I stayed in Athens for two months. I had already given some money to the smugglers to cross the border. I had some left from the sale of my car, but paying for rent and food, soon I had run out of money. I started working as an Uber driver at night. A friend was using the car during the day and I was taking it at night. As it goes in a proverb: "It doesn't matter who you were in the past. What matters is who you will turn into, in the future." How correct this was! Yesterday, I was a well-known scientist receiving prestigious awards; and now I was an Uber driver who took refuge with the Greek people; the very same people who had been depicted to us as monsters for so long. During this entire time period, I had gone through so many traumas. Nevertheless, despite all the challenges, I was thankful to my Lord, who was helping and protecting us in different ways.

WITH DEAR FRIENDS AGAIN

Since my wife was a German citizen, our family reunion process did not take so long. The German university where I previously received my Ph.D. also supported us. They sent a letter to the Greek Embassy stating: "He's our former student, he will work here as soon as he gets here." Why were they taking care of me? Well, they had seen my research on scientific publication platforms and they had thought: "This is our student and a successful scientist. We have to take care of him." Scientists in Western countries were appreciated and they were given their due. They would only laugh if they heard a person to be declared a terrorist just because he was reading the books of someone or had an account in a bank. What's more, when I was in prison, the same German university offered to send a lawyer for me, but my wife replied that it wouldn't be appropriate, given the circumstances. In Turkey, things were handled not according to the rule of law, but with hatred and grudge; it would be against my case if foreign countries intervened for me. The president of Turkey was already making baseless claims that those who studied abroad were agents and spies working for those countries. Turkey's foundations were shaken by these policies that had no basis in reality.

It was July 5, 2018, when I went to Germany for freedom and to reunite with my family. Many years ago, I had come from Germany to Turkey with joy and hopes, but now I had left Turkey, crying and suffering from so much pain. I thanked God for being able to hug my children again. I was finding consolation in knowing that I would soon start working as an academician in Germany, the job that I had lost during the massacre of justice in Turkey, which they had called the KHK (Government Decree Law).

Just a month later, on August 1, 2018, I was hired by the University of Giessen, where I had previously received my Ph.D. degree. If I say I was greeted with drum rolls, it would not be an exaggeration. The university authorities had prepared a welcome party. The President of the university, the deans, and so many faculty members were there for me. I had my academic identity again. I could have a house now, furniture, and a car; but most importantly, I had my job back, my dignity, my honor. I was grateful to the German government. That welcome party was like a cure for my damaged honor and dignity. I was like a child who was receiving love and attention from strangers but not from his immediate family. I was both happy and sad at the same time. I don't know if this feeling will ever pass. A part of me will always be bitter and resentful.

The university president made me a member of a club of distinguished professors and presented my membership card at the party. They announced that they would support my work on the development of that particular drug that was needed by humanity. They pretty much saved me from those people who had condemned me for crimes I didn't commit, and they gave my reputation back to me, in standing ovation. There are no words to describe my feelings. I only pray that "God willing, I will not embarrass these nice people and I will do great things in the name of science."

I now continue with my project on the use of the substance 'X' for rapid recovery of bone fractures. Meanwhile, I've also progressed a lot in my studies on skeletal system disorders, breast cancer, and skin cancer. My efforts since I came here one and a half year ago are finally bearing fruit. My scientific article has been accepted in a journal belonging to the Nature group and it will be published in a few weeks.

I am constantly thinking about why I've been through all of this. Why all these atrocities and destructions are still going on in Turkey? I can't speak for others but for myself, I'm trying to understand the divine wisdom behind all this. Perhaps God wanted me to continue with my research where there were more opportunities and resources. I don't know. I am now watching the ongoing fire from a distance, the fire in which I was a few years ago. I pray for all the oppressed people who are left behind, who can't leave Turkey.

A person who went through immense sufferings can never be the same person again. Yes, a lot has changed after the night of the coup. I've changed. I've been so broken by what I've been through, to the extent that my entire balance and perception has changed. The persecution I have been through in my own country and the righteousness and kindness I have seen at people from other nationalities and religions, has taught me a lot. My heart has expanded; my love has grown; my perspective has changed. The blows I had unjustly received have shattered my prejudices. I've learned to evaluate people not by their beliefs but by their morals. I perceive life and events more universally now. For a believer, everyone is a servant of God and is so precious. And as for homeland, the whole world is our homeland, I understand it better now. I wish God will grant me His blessing to serve my homeland and the entire humanity until my last breath.

2

DIAMONDS
IN TRASH

As told by Yakup Y.

You know how it goes in fairy tales... The dark sorcerer who gets angry at the prince uses magic to turn him into a frog. The frog-turned-prince cannot talk anymore, so only a miracle can save him now. This is pretty much what happened to the volunteers of the Hizmet Movement. Using a staged fake coup, the patriots in Turkey were framed in just one night as traitors by the evil corrupt political power and their names were added into the lists of torture and death. All their properties have been seized and they were left no other choice but to escape from their homeland.

What you will read below is a true story of a Hizmet volunteer, one of the lawyers of Bank Asya. You will witness how his life has been taken from him after that ominous night of coup and how he fought back to save his family from evil.

The only difference between this story and those fairy tales is that... everything in this story is true!

Zeynep Kayadelen

If you are fighting darkness, dream of the sunrise!

DIAMONDS IN TRASH

SMILE OF DESTINY

If you have a story to tell, you must have endured pain in your past. Much of what we know of human history is full of incredible pain and suffering. Tragedies and sufferings should be recorded and conveyed to future generations so that they may learn how difficult it is to walk the road of pain and how that pain transforms a person and leads him eventually to the inner core of his personality. After all, what is the purpose of a human but finding his true self and place in this world?

I was born in 1983 in Malatya, Turkey. Well, you can call me Yakup. At the age of 37, I already feel as if I am 100 years old. All the injustice and cruelty that I have been exposed to wore out my heart so much that I grew old at a young age.

My childhood was quite difficult. Not only we lived in poverty, but also my father didn't pay too much attention to us, either. I don't remember spending time with him in my childhood, he used to stay out until late in the night and would spend his income in nightlife. In his eyes, we were no more than some strangers that he had to live with together. My mother, on the other hand, was quite religious and had a peaceful character. There was a cliff between my parents, and I was trying to find something to hold on around that cliff, for myself and my siblings.

Destiny smiled on me when I graduated from the elementary school in the city of Kahramanmaras where we were living. I was enrolled in a private school, run by Hizmet movement, with the mediation of some family friends. I was a bright and hard-working student, so I got a full scholarship. I always had a passion for knowledge, and that school was the best place that I could be at. This is how I first met with Hizmet movement, which has since then become the source of many blessings in my life.

There were hostilities and conflicts going on in the country, but I was only a kid and didn't understand much about them. When I got older, things have made more sense. In the 1990s, religious people in Turkey were being oppressed, just like the political persecution of the people who are opposing the government now. The government had enacted a mandatory eight-year education policy and by doing so aimed to shut down the religious schools. Since the high school branch of my private school was also shut down, I transferred to a public school. I was so sad since I had to leave my school, and on top of that on the first day in the new school, nine classmates of mine and I were beaten by the deputy principal, as a welcoming gesture (!)

Looking back now, that private school of Hizmet was a true blessing for a kid like me coming from a poor family living in an underdeveloped region of the country. The classrooms in the school were state of the art, but what is more important is that everything I learned in life in terms of morality, I had learned them in that school. Yes, I was a bright and hard-working student, but it was that school which let me appreciate learning and knowledge and which pushed me to do my absolute best. I will be forever grateful to that Hizmet school.

After I had transferred to the public school, I soon had realized that I couldn't follow my dreams there and decided to leave that school and applied to another Hizmet school in the city of Gaziantep. I talked to the deputy principal of the school and got a bargain on the tuition. To pay the tuition, I sold my computer and also found a student loan. It was a boarding school so during my entire high school years I was away from my family. Meanwhile, I was working in the school cafeteria and even sending some money to my mother back home. During my high school years, my parents never attended any parent-teacher conferences. When I had graduated, I had a full scholarship and the highest GPA in the entire school. I couldn't realize it then at that young age but apparently, every action in life had a consequence and even a smallest effort would not go in vain. Sometimes you could lose your hope, but if you were to keep making an effort, new doors eventually would open in front of you.

After high school, I took the national university entrance exam in 2002. With the very high score I received, I could get admission into any public university's law school. But I aimed higher and decided to study international law in Bilkent University, which was one of the most prestigious private universities in Turkey. Actually, I had taken a big risk; after all, my family was pretty poor and most of the students in Bilkent were coming from very rich families. But I didn't care. There were days when I didn't have any money to eat a decent meal. But eventually, I graduated successfully from the university in 2006. I couldn't afford a cap and gown, so I decided not to attend the graduation ceremony. One of my friends insisted to lend me money and I accepted. After the ceremony was over, everyone was hugging their parents and family members. I was standing there by myself, all alone. I had no family member around me to share that special moment. One of my classmates was kind enough to introduce me to his parents, they congratulated me and invited me to have pictures taken together.

Surely, nothing happens in life without a purpose. There is a famous saying: "What doesn't kill you makes you stronger." Well, I don't totally agree with this statement, but there is certainly some truth to it. Yes, I was deprived of a family warmth and support, but I had used this as an extra motivation for me to study even harder and get ahead of other students.

I had set big goals to accomplish, for myself and my country. In the Hizmet schools, we had learned how to work for the betterment of the entire humanity and universal peace. To accomplish these goals, I decided to continue with my postgraduate education in France, following the advice of my professors in Bilkent. I had a successful academic career in France for five years. There has always been a shortage of jurists in Turkey who had literacy in a foreign language, and I had now professional proficiency in two foreign languages: English and French.

ALAS! LONGING FOR HOMELAND

The sad truth is that all the sufferings in my life were due to my love and ambition for my homeland. I was living in Europe, I could easily build a very comfortable future for me, but yet in 2011, I returned back to Turkey. I was going to serve my people in my own country. I started my career working as a government employee in Ankara, the capital city. Being proficient in law, English, and French I was helping several government offices with their affairs. Working hard, I was hoping that I could change a few things in order to improve the lives of the poor people living in the rural communities. It didn't take too long for me to figure out that I was wrong. The wheels of government bureaucracy were turning so slowly and inefficiently, and I was pretty insignificant in this giant organization of government. If I were selfish, if my goal were to get into some high-rank office eventually, that would be easy. I could do that by simply saying "Yes Sir", by not taking any risk, and by pleasing the egos of my superiors. But that political hypocrisy was not for me. So many wrongdoings were being committed and so many problems lingered without any solution for so long, and I could do nothing but watch that vicious circle which was slowly engulfing me. I was so disappointed, that was not what I had dreamed of. I couldn't waste my time and knowledge like that, I had to come up with a decision.

After a while, I quit my job as a bureaucrat, which was a dream job for many people living in Turkey. I opened a law office with a few partners together and started working as a lawyer. We were providing international law expertise in five languages. It didn't take too long for our law office to be well known in the international law affairs. One of our clients was the financial institution Bank Asya, which was affiliated with Hizmet movement. Our law office was taking care of all the international affairs of Bank Asya. We helped to establish significant trade relations with many firms in several African countries.

Throughout my career, I have been close to the Hizmet movement. In particular, I was contributing in the education sector by providing scholarships to students in need. I had gone through so many difficulties during my school years so I wanted to ease up at least a few students' hardships. While working as a bureaucrat, I had seen clearly that education was the most important factor for the social and economic development of a nation. As much as political hypocrisy was a poison, its antidote was an educated nation. Investing in education meant investing in the future and development. I was wholeheartedly supporting education activities of the Hizmet movement, which originated in Turkey like a pure fresh source of water and then flowed in all directions around the world like an exuberant river. After all, the education I had received in my school years was due to the generous voluntary contributions of altruistic people.

Everything was going well in my life. How could I know then that there were huge troubles waiting in the near future? But of course, calamities don't make an appointment before showing up on your doorstep, do they? Life is indeed a bundle of miracles, and one does not properly appreciate all the blessings in life. We take things for granted and don't realize that this world has two sides, just like a mirror. One side is shiny and bright, the other side is coated with a dark substance. Soon I was to meet the dark side…

In the meantime, I was married in 2012. My spouse had attended a Hizmet school too, like me, even if for a while. We had a happy marriage and shortly after we had a baby. However, I didn't have a good relationship with my wife's mother. She was not approving of my religious way of life, neither my closeness to Hizmet movement.

Everything seemed to be going smoothly in Turkey for the last few years. There was a visible economic development across the country. Military coups, chaos, and internal conflicts seemed to be all left behind. But apparently, a devastating storm was at the door, while we were expecting sunny days to continue. It was around 2012 when the ruling AKP government started to take a stance against the Hizmet movement. We were to learn later that the reason for this was that the bribery and corruption of the government was being investigated and exposed by some officials who were close to Hizmet movement.

Actually, it was not something new in the recent history of Turkey that the ruling government and secularist military was acting against religious people. There has been always a deep organization and alliance against the unified spirit of the nation. That organization was provoking different groups in the country and creating chaos every now and then, for so many decades. But this time, they were staging even a bigger and much better-planned plot against innocent people. They were pretty much trying to isolate and exterminate the religious people and other opposition groups in the country using the AKP government which was known to be *apparently* promoting religion. A heinous plan, unlike anything seen before, was already on the move.

Our law firm was among the first targets of the government's rage against the Hizmet movement, right after the government's corruption scandal[14] was exposed in December 2013. One of our clients was Kaynak Holding and another was Bank Asya. Both institutions were established mostly by donations of the volunteers in the Hizmet movement. Our law firm got its share from the defamatory media coverage which was getting widespread nationwide. Several government-controlled newspapers were making fabricated news about the partners of our law firm. Those newspapers were full of daily lies and slanders about the Hizmet movement. Their sole purpose was to discredit the movement in the public eye. We

---

14   The December 17-25, 2013 corruption scandal in Turkey refers to a criminal investigation that involves several key people in the Turkish government. Prosecutors accused 14 people, including several family members of the cabinet ministers, Suleyman Aslan, the director of state-owned bank (Halkbank) and Turkish-Iranian businessman Reza Zarrab, of bribery, corruption, fraud, money laundering and gold smuggling. In March 2016, Reza Zarrab was arrested in Miami. In November 2017, Zarrab cooperated with federal prosecutors and has become key witness in the case of money laundering and violating sanctions on Iran.

didn't know then that apparently they were setting the ground for the big strike that was soon to occur. A mass media under full control was indeed any dictator's absolute necessity. Being caught red-handed in December 17/25 corruption probes, the government decided to cooperate with the deep state terrorist groups to defame Hizmet movement and eradicate it. When my partners were being accused of made-up charges against them, the so-called "coup-attempt" had not happened yet. Two of my partners were arrested after a police raid to their houses. After they were released, they left the law firm and the country. I was extremely sad and nervous; all we had established was being demolished step by step.

Like an anaconda leaving its prey breathless before devouring, all the institutions of the Hizmet movement were being seized by the government illegally. I was in shock as a lawyer to see that the government itself was at the center of the illegal and unconstitutional activities. Just when we were thinking that we reached a certain level of democracy in the country, the democracy had turned into mobocracy. Beyond all, it was really sad to see no sign of disapproval in the society against all the injustice they were witnessing against the Hizmet movement. After all, hundreds of thousands of people had got a good education in Hizmet institutions since decades ago. It was simply ungratefulness, nothing else.

In February 2015, the government, through Savings Deposit Insurance Fund[15], had confiscated 63% of the shares of Bank

---

15   The Savings Deposit Insurance Fund of Turkey (Turkish: Tasarruf Mevduatı Sigorta

Asya, on the grounds of allegedly missing to declare some financial information. Four months later, with the excuse of some missing documents from 30 out of 185 shareholders, the government seized all the shares. I had been providing judicial support for the international finances of the bank and have continued to do so for a while after the seizure by the government.

Shortly after, one morning I couldn't enter the headquarters of the bank I worked for, as they had deactivated my ID card. Security personnel was standing in front of me like a wall. People whom I had been greeting every morning, were looking at me as if I was a stranger. I cannot forget how despised I felt while turning back from the door that day. That treatment which I never deserved had erased all my trust towards the government. I was not safe anymore, I felt as if I had just entered in a minefield.

Another shock was waiting for me soon. An executive officer in the bank, whom I had considered as a friend for a long time, seized my payroll balance in the bank. It was the payment for the law service that I was providing to the bank. They were pretty much saying: "We are not giving your money to you, and there is nothing you can do about it!" That was so unfair and against the law. But since I had been observing how the entire judicial system was going on a slippery slope, I did not sue them. I tried to obtain a writ of execution but failed. It was extremely demoralizing not to be able

---

Fonu, TMSF) is the governing body concerned with matters of fund management and insurance in the Turkish banking system. More than 1,000 companies with a total value of tens of billions dollars in assets have been seized by the government and then transferred to TMSF since July 15, 2016.

---

to ask for your own rights despite being a lawyer. The psychological burden of that was beyond words, I was feeling as if I was being suffocated.

In retrospect, we were not aware of the final theater act written for us and were hoping in vain that the rule of law would be eventually established, and all this mob rule would end. Meanwhile, the government was confiscating everything which belonged to the volunteers of the Hizmet movement by appointing a government trustee to hundreds of firms and institutions. I knew how to endure poverty and many different hardships in life, but I had no idea how to handle such lawlessness and tyranny.

I was wounded and hurt, but I was more worried and concerned for my country. What makes a group of people a polity under a system of governance was the rule of law. Yet, we were getting rid of the rule of law. The Erdogan government was enacting a new decree every morning, bypassing the Parliament. Everything was turned upside down. I hoped and prayed for a long time that people of reason could have objected to all this nonsense. Alas! That never happened. And then, one night the entire country has chosen to jump off the cliff. When they were falling from the cliff, they were cheering with a laugh of victory. It was a night of suicide, when death was portrayed as heroism and salvation. It was the Friday night of July 15, 2016.

HOW ABOUT THOSE TRUCKS?

That night of July 15, 2016 was a breakpoint for Turkey. It was as if a dark-hearted witch put the entire nation under a black magic. All the colors of life faded and dark ominous clouds surrounded us. The whole country turned into a mourning house.

It is a famous saying: "We were busy making plans; forgetting God has other plans too." That night we were at a concert in Istanbul with my wife, to relax after a busy week, completely unaware of things to happen. It was around 10 p.m. when a restlessness started in the concert hall. Looking at the news using my phone, I learned that the Bosphorus Bridge was closed, and the soldiers were on the streets. Everybody in the concert hall was trying to figure out what was going on. As the unrest intensified, the concert ended. Just like that, the normalcy had ended in the entire country. As if a virus had infected people secretly, most of the nation would turn into a kind of zombie that night. The next morning, there were thousands of fake heroes, bogus stories of bravery, and fabricated traitors…

After the concert ended abruptly, the audience started to leave the concert hall with eyes full of worry and fear. Everybody was in shock. My wife and I went to a friend's house which was close by and turned the TV on. Indeed, there was an ongoing military coup attempt. I froze for a moment, just like a patient who heard from his doctor that he had a terminal cancer. I couldn't believe what I was seeing. News anchors on TV were calling out to the public: "Everybody leave their homes! Rush to occupy streets! Resist the coup!" I had never watched a coup live on TV before, but I think that was not how a military coup was supposed to be. I could sense that something different was going on behind the scenes. Erdogan, the president and the leader of the ruling party AKP, had announced on live TV that the Hizmet movement was behind the coup and they would bring the movement to account. My wife was so afraid. I was mostly preoccupied with the question: "What will happen to us?" We were so confused and sad. There were so many questions in my head: Why? How? With a chill running down our spines, we watched the unfolding events on TV for a couple of hours.

We had left our son at my mother-in-law's place in Bakirkoy. We decided to leave our friend's house to go there as soon as possible. Probably it was a parental reflex to first secure the family members during a disastrous moment. We were being pulled into a fight without knowing anything about it or how long will it last. It was like a nightmare I was trying to wake up from, yet sinking deeper as I struggled.

We first tried to go to Bakirkoy over Maslak. But since the roads were closed by demonstrators, we had to change our route. All the lights of the buildings around were on. The streets were full of chaos. The main roads were closed by hundreds of trucks belonging to the municipality. The coup had started only a few hours ago. How could those hundreds of trucks be organized in such a short amount of time against the coup? It didn't make sense. It looked like many things were planned beforehand, as if some people knew that a coup attempt would occur in the evening and they had already made plans against it. Since the main roads were all blocked, people were pretty much forced to stay on the streets. Streets were full of hundreds of thousands of people, and gunshots were heard from here and there. It was almost impossible for us to drive such a short distance to Bakirkoy and get our son. Much later, a friend living on the Anatolian side of the city told me that it was pretty much the same situation over there too, the trucks had blocked all the main roads there, as well.

Driving an SUV, I tried to move forward even if I had to go over sidewalks and raised medians. We finally reached my mother-in-law's house and spent the rest of the night praying and hoping for the best. That extremely gloomy night ended eventually. But the darkness of that night has been over the entire country since.

We were so worried all night long, it was difficult to foresee whether this coup attempt would result in a civil unrest or not. When and how would all this chaos end? If you had never lived such a political and social chaos in your country, it would be very difficult for you to understand how it all feels. The state was like a parent to us, this is how the entire nation was raised. On that night we were all like small children seeing their parents in agony. Fighter jets were flying so low and they were making such a loud noise that the windows of the nearby buildings were all shaking. All the mosques were broadcasting religious hymns outside until morning hours. It was as if the entire nation was somehow teleported in the middle of a war. We were unprotected and unprepared. I was feeling that same spine-chilling horror just like I felt when my drunk father had come home years ago and threatened my mom with a knife.

All news outlets were claiming that the coup attempt was organized by Hizmet movement followers. My wife had not said anything about it yet, but I could see that she was looking at me in a different way. As a lawyer, I was familiar with many unfounded and unlawful claims against my clients last couple of years, but the claim of "organizing a coup" was not something easy to overcome.

That time period taught me one more fact: If there is a dictator in a country, there also exists an environment and public which creates and supports him. Neither a rose can grow without proper setting nor a thorn. It was incomprehensible and terrifying how the Turkish nation got worked up so easily without questioning or analyzing the ongoing events. I witnessed so many things on that night which could only be described as public frenzy. People who have only been concerned with drugs and alcohol in their lives were now turned into some kind of "patriots" looking for traitors to butcher them on the streets. People were ready to do anything, they had found an excuse to discharge the hatred and hostility which was boiling inside them for some time. They were supposedly protecting the country and state. Even the most reasonable-looking ones among them had rushed the very next day to look around for a Hizmet volunteer and report him to the police.

Like my wife, my mother-in-law had also changed her attitude towards me right after that night. She was constantly grumbling. I could have said: "Look, I was together with you all the time and I have no idea whatsoever about what is going on. I didn't commit a crime!" But whatever I would have said would not matter. She didn't like me anyhow and now she had an excuse. Shortly after, we went to our own house.

The following days the nightmare continued. The official story was, supposedly Hizmet volunteers had attempted a coup, killed innocent people, but the coup attempt was not successful. That was nonsense! They were saying that for 40 years Hizmet movement has secretly infiltrated all the government and military offices, brainwashed thousands of people, only to plot such a sloppy coup to seize the power and to fail in a few hours! However absurd it may sound, that story was bought by so many, and only because they were in dire need of such a story. We now had heroes who lay down in front of military tanks and stopped the traitors by jamming tank exhaust pipes with their undershirts! All over the country, there was an eager patriotic ritual such as keeping all-night-watch in the public squares of the cities, decorating everywhere with flags, and cursing Hizmet volunteers day and night. So many hoodlums made up stories about how they fought against the coup on that night, just to get some money award from the government. The crazier things you would do to show your loyalty, the more patriotic you would be considered. If your car did not display any Turkish flag, you could be stopped while driving and beaten up violently. I absolutely loved my country, but I wouldn't display a flag on my car just because of that frenzy. It is difficult to grasp it, but if you had not displayed a flag on a window in your house, you would be reported to the police as a terrorist. Hizmet movement had a new name after that night: FETO[16] terror organization. That was the name given by the government. Probably this was the first time that the name of a terrorist organization was chosen by the government!

We were mistaken to assume that it was the Erdogan government who was oppressing us and the society would one day object to all this injustice. Yet, it was the society who was approving whatever the government was telling them without any objection. That night of the coup and the following days showed how deep the ethical erosion was in Turkey, and how it went unnoticed for a long time. As they say in Germany: "If there's a Nazi at the table and 10 other people sitting there talking to him, actually there are 11 Nazis at the table." That was pretty much summarizing our situation. The government was abandoning all the rules of law and the public was applauding them with cheers and shouting: "Good job! Keep up the good work!"

---

16   A so-called terrorist organization, referred as such only by the Erdogan Government in Turkey, otherwise known as Gulen movement or Hizmet (Service) movement worldwide, a transnational civil society initiative that advocates for the ideals of human rights, equal opportunity, democracy, non-violence and the emphatic acceptance of religious and cultural diversity. For more information: www.afsv.org

My closeness to the Hizmet movement was known by the people around me. Right after the night of the coup, everyone cut their contact with me. My close friends started to see me as a terrorist, no one called me or answered my calls. When the police raided my third partner's home after a week from the coup, I clearly realized that there was no right of life for us in Turkey anymore. I booked a plane ticket immediately as I would not wait for the government cops to come and arrest me. I packed up my personal belongings. Meanwhile, I looked inside each room carefully and removed all the books related to Hizmet movement and put them into boxes, with tears in my eyes.

Illustrated by A.B.

DIMONDS AND TRASH

Those familiar with Istanbul would know that there is not too much difference between day and night in terms of heat and humidity, especially in the summer. That July night was one like that. My shirt was soaked in sweat and beads of sweat were trickling down my face. But the main reason was not the heat and humidity, I was extremely stressed out because the trunk of the car was full of books and if I were caught that would be sufficient for me to spend a long time in prison. All the books in the trunk were considered to be "crime evidence" by the government. The contents of the books were all related to peace and love, but it didn't matter. They were written by Fethullah Gulen[17] and Hizmet volunteers and published by Hizmet affiliated publishing companies, and that was consider a crime (!). I really didn't want to but I had to get rid of them as soon as possible and without being noticed by anyone. It was so sad that everywhere in Turkey, thousands of books were burned, thrown away into dumpsters, or buried in the ground.

I parked slowly next to a garbage dumpster under the streetlight

---

17   Fethullah Gulen is an Islamic scholar, preacher and social advocate, whose decades-long commitment to education, altruistic community service, and interfaith harmony has inspired millions in Turkey and around the world. Described as one of the world's most important Muslim figures, Gulen has reinterpreted aspects of Islamic tradition to meet the needs of contemporary Muslims. He has dedicated his life to interfaith and intercultural dialogue, community service and providing access to quality education. For more information, please visit www.afsv.org

and observed the surrounding for some time before getting off the car. The entire city was buzzing like a sick person in deep pain, siren sounds coming from far away. I quickly got off my car, grabbed one of the two boxes in the trunk, dropped it into the dumpster, and left the scene as fast as possible. I drove randomly for another five minutes and stopped next to another dumpster. Just when I was about to drop the second box into the dumpster, the cardboard was torn apart and the books fell down. Afraid of being caught red-handed, I checked around first to make sure that nobody saw me. When I kneeled down to get the books, I noticed the cover of one of them had the title: "Diamond Series." These books written by Fethullah Gulen were to guide the readers on their path to self-awareness, promoting love and peace, and rejecting any form of terrorism. How terribly sad it was to see that these books were now labeled as evidence for terror! I looked at the books one last time, then I looked at the dumpster and the city. To label these books as evidence of terror, and to arrest people because they had these books of love and peace was itself the terror. Just how confused was the entire society? How did the entire country come to this point? I was so heart-stricken and burst into tears. With tears running down my face, I grabbed the books and threw them into the dumpster, and quickly drove away...

It didn't matter who said what, Hizmet movement had not deserved this treatment. I knew first-hand all the good they have done for the entire society. In my personal life story, this movement was like a father to me, when my own father neglected me. It was like a mother to me, when my own mother wanted to be next to me, but she simply couldn't. I was the example and witness of how this movement had been like a guarding parent to thousands and thousands of people who were lost like me. No individual or no movement is perfect and flawless. But I am absolutely sure that Hizmet volunteers would never ever grab guns and go to the streets for a coup. No way! Besides, and just hypothetically, even if some people from the Hizmet movement had participated in the coup attempt, why would I be blamed for that? What happened to the principle of individual criminal responsibility[18]?

There were no other "criminal books" (!) left in my trunk. My flight was the next morning. We went to my in-laws' house. I had brought the paper shredder from the office. We gathered all the books there and shredded any sort of publication that might be related to Hizmet. My wife's family found it very odd, saying: "That's nonsense! Why would someone be arrested just because of a book?" They were somehow denying things and events which were unfolding in front of their eyes, that was really weird. I had told them many times that I had nothing to do with the coup attempt and the only crime (!) I had committed was reading books and newspapers which were published by the Hizmet movement and which were promoting peace and love! It was impossible to explain

---

18   Turkish Panel code, Article 20/1: Criminal responsibility is personal. No one shall be deemed culpable for the conduct of another.

and convince them that the Hizmet movement had nothing to do with the coup attempt or all the other alleged crimes. Their whole argument was pretty much this: "Our government wouldn't run after people if they were not guilty." It wouldn't matter how many times you explain, they don't and they won't understand.

I went also to my sister's house on the same night to say goodbye and to *clean* her house too. That night, I had cleaned three houses from so many books related to religion, ethics, culture, and literature. I gathered many books and journals in my sister's house and threw them into various dumpsters around the city. It was not only books that I was throwing into dumpsters, but it was also my hope and belief in this country and my joy of living. My heart felt empty and ice cold. Everything which was connecting me to my homeland was breaking off with every teardrop I shed. Anatolian land, that I was in love with since my childhood, had turned into a dark valley where evil screams for "blood, revenge, and death" were echoing. I was no longer able to recognize people. I was a complete stranger now, and it was impossible for someone to keep his mind and heart clean and healthy in this setting of frenzy. Actually, it was kind of tragicomic because most of the books that they had declared crime evidence were about Islam and its message of peace, and it was the Erdogan government which was supposedly protecting Islam. Those claiming to serve and protect Islam were now considering the books about Islam as crime evidence! How bizarre it was! They were oppressing the God-fearing people in the name of God. The names of God and His Messengers were only on their lips and not in their hearts. Their words and actions were so cruel that they had nothing to do with any kind of belief system, whatsoever. Religion was for them a useful tool to manipulate masses of people. To label and show the innocent people as terrorists was so easy for them, it was sufficient to give a speech about religion and patriotism, and then just point their fingers at those innocent people and shout: "These are traitors and infidels!". Masses of the so-called patriots were waiting to find those so-called traitors and harm them in any way. It was their patriotic duty (!) to harm those traitors.

They did so much evil in the name of Islam. One of the consequences has been many people losing their faith and even despising the religion. The whole nation was burning now with the arsonist fire lit in that night. What was the real reason beyond all this chaos? Would we know one day who had plotted all this madness? I believe wholeheartedly, we will learn sooner or later who planned the coup attempt and why they victimized Hizmet.

By the way, I want to put it on record that those people with black gowns and long beards and who call themselves Muslims but support many different terrorist activities all over the world in the name of Islam are indeed the biggest enemies of Islam. Islam is not a religion of killing and annihilating. It is a religion of peace and life, to live and let live.

If some books are burned in a country for a reason, definitely it is that very same "reason" which is guilty. History is full of examples of that, from Mongol invasion to the Soviets to the Nazis, they all burned and destroyed books at the early stages of forming their cruel systems. Similarly in Turkey, during recent years, tens of thousands copies of many books have been thrown away, burnt, or hidden. This alone is enough to show the cruelty of the regime in Turkey.

Following the controversial July 15 coup attempt, the rule of law was suspended and the judiciary became fully unfunctional as an independent entity. The government clearly evolved into a dictatorship. I was in constant traumatic shock and my psychology was broken. I had a law degree, my job was to help people seeking justice, but now it was all in vain. What was the law degree good for when the rule of law was no more? All my efforts had gone futile.

I have witnessed how many people have changed in the aftermath of the coup, either for a reward or due to fear. My closest friends were behaving as if I was a complete stranger. Apparently, we had put too much trust in the Turkish people. We were unfortunately raised with the tale of the Turkish nation being one of the best in the world. However, it was not the race or color which was adding value, but it was the mercy and virtue in the heart. I was now able to see it one more time clearly. I witnessed so many people rushing to report their own children, siblings, and colleagues to the police as hizmet members, and to get a share of their confiscated property. We might have been living in such a swamp but had not noticed it until then. I am still so disgusted with all those things that I have witnessed. An invisible hand woke us up from that deep sleep. When I look back now, I am grateful for waking up from that illusion no matter how bitter the truth was that we faced. Yes, our world was destroyed. I was either going to find a new place to live... or leave me and my loved ones to the mercy of those tyrants. I had decided to leave that land of oppression.

My wife and I left my sister's home early morning for the airport. Our transit flight was to the U.S. over Germany. I was extremely anxious. There was an ongoing witch hunt all over the country and I could have been arrested in the airport without any reason. I was known as the lawyer working for the Hizmet affiliated institutions, but anyone could be arrested for any reason, anyhow. Friends and spouses were reporting each other to the police as Hizmet member just because they had a quarrel with each other. The government was continuously sending text messages to our cellphones asking to report people affiliated with Hizmet movement to the police. Photos and videos of tortured people under custody were shared in every media outlet. People were beaten up on streets. As I was driving to the airport, I was trying to prepare myself for every possible scenario that could happen.

I was a lawyer who always defended the rights of others and only wanted their wellbeing. But now, I was trying to find a place to hide as if I was an outlaw and a terrorist. I was hoping to leave the country without being noticed at a checkpoint by someone in love with their beloved dictator.

On the night of the coup attempt, tens of thousands of ordinary people were minding their own business or were in a concert like us and they had nothing to do with the coup whatsoever, yet they were labeled as traitors and putschists. I didn't curse on the day I returned from France years ago to this country, but I cursed on the ungratefulness and ignorance of the people living in this country. How come they had become so blind and ignorant to the facts? Would they not know at all what a real terrorist organization looked like, and who would be called a traitor? As I said earlier, it was not only my books that I had thrown into the dumpster, but also all my good feelings and love about this country and its people. And now I was leaving, deeply heartbroken.

THE TRUTH WILL ULTIMATELY PREVAIL

On the way to airport, we changed our plans. It would be a better idea if I were to leave the country alone and my wife would follow me a few days later. We couldn't take our son with us due to some passport problems. There were so many police officers at every checkpoint outside and inside the airport. If they were to notice anyone walking a bit faster or acting suspiciously, they were stopping him and asking questions. We had to remain so calm. There was no room for even the smallest hesitation. If I were arrested, they could have arrested my wife, too. It was not unusual to arrest the spouses, children, or siblings of the Hizmet volunteers, just due to their kinship. There was no more rule of law. The government and its police were acting with hatred and not with the law. Against the Hizmet movement, they had launched the hatred movement. Hate was such a dark feeling, it wouldn't leave any room for rationale, logic, and mercy. In my opinion, someone whose heart is full of hatred is an insane person. The volunteers of the hatred movement were looking for someone to hunt. The ruling party AKP and some of its followers were no different than primitive savages. The government had even enacted decree laws to protect the murderers of innocent people on the night of the coup attempt: "A citizen won't be held responsible because of the bloodshed they caused while trying to stop the coup." Stones were tied and rabid dogs loose.

Only five years ago, I had returned to my country from Europe with big dreams and aspirations, and now I was leaving again, with a broken heart, towards uncertainty. When you depart from someone or someplace, you bring something along with you just to comfort your heart and to feel strong. In my case, and thousands of other people's cases, our hearts were empty, ice-cold, deeply broken. We were leaving our country behind because our country had left us in the hands of tyrants.

Could this all be real? It was so difficult to believe. Denial was one of the basic responses to a shock. Storms were raging inside me, yet I was like a walking dead. At the checkpoint, I handed my passport to the officer. When he asked what my profession was, I replied "lawyer." The officer shockingly informed me there was an executive order prohibiting the lawyers, prosecutors, and judges from leaving the country. This was obviously against the law; how could they impose a travel ban on the basis of profession? I insisted on showing all the arrival and departure stamps in my passport and saying: "My job is international; I have to take this flight." He cross-checked my name both from the computer and from a list of names in front of him. He also inquired with his superior several times. Apparently, there was a red list of names that he was looking at. That list must have had the names of the regular citizens turned so-called "terrorists" overnight. They were normal ordinary citizens, for otherwise, if they had any criminal record, police would not need such a list anyhow. I was really trying my best to remain calm. How could a government deem such treatment suitable for its citizens?

Minutes were passing while I was waiting at the checkpoint. Different police officers came by, talked to each other, checked various other lists prepared by the intelligence department. It was impossible for the lawyer of the Bank Asya not to be on their lists. As a matter of fact, I had learned later that two days before I had been to the airport, an arrest warrant had been issued for me. But somehow, my name was not on their list. That was truly a divine intervention from God. Eventually, they let me pass the final checkpoint. The officer who stamped my passport said: "I shouldn't let you pass but, anyhow." When I boarded the plane, I had to feel happy, but I was so exhausted emotionally. Not so long ago, if someone would have told me these things would happen soon, I would probably think he was crazy. But I was going through it firsthand now.

I had not informed anyone that I was leaving Turkey. Only my sister and my wife knew it. My wife had gone to her mother's house after dropping me off at the airport. I called her after I passed the last checkpoint. Her mom was shouting at the background, "Traitors! They destroyed our country, now they run away!" I gulped sadly. These pro-government people could just not see whose lives were getting destroyed. Was it not me who had lost his everything? Was it not me whose life was taken away from him? My mother-in-law was shouting many other insulting words. I am sure if she could, she would happily let me arrested, too.

Those days taught me that not all fugitives were guilty. When a wolf was chasing a lamb, it would be foolish for the lamb to turn back and ask mercy from the wolf. If there were a small sign of mercy or justice, I would not hesitate to ask for it. But I was a lawyer and I had watched how justice was trampled upon and raped recently, and by the very same people who had sworn to protect it. They were obviously using the phrase "running away" in an insulting way, but running away was not only my right, but it was also my responsibility.

When the plane was flying over Istanbul my eyes welled up with tears. Only God knows when I would see again the poetic beauty of that city. When would I eat simit[19] under the screams of seagulls? The cheers of my childhood were still echoing in the streets of my hometown, and now I could only dream about them. Aside from all my properties and earnings, they had taken my country away from me! And why? For the sake of what? I had not done anything wrong or illegal. They had ruined not only the lives of hundreds of thousands of innocent people like me but also the entire nation. Think about it, can a country gain anything when it declares war against its own judges, prosecutors, military officers, and ordinary citizens?

---

19   Simit is a circular bread, typically encrusted with sesame seeds or, less commonly, poppy, flax or sunflower seeds. It is widely known as Turkish bagel in the United States.

SEPARATION UPON SEPARATION

I arrived in the U.S. on the 23rd of July 2016. My wife's brother was living in the U.S. and thankfully he hosted me in their house. Three days after I arrived, the workplace of my wife was also shut down with a decree-law. The government was bypassing the Parliament and using decree-laws to shut down businesses, fire people, confiscate their properties, and imprison them. My wife came to the U.S. four days after me. Her only tie with the Hizmet movement was being married to me. The managers of the institution she worked for had some closeness to Hizmet. Therefore, she was also at the risk of being imprisoned. If you greeted someone who had greeted someone else, and if that someone else had committed a crime, that was enough evidence for your crime of abetment. My wife had applied for our son's passport but had to leave the country before his passport was issued. Our little son had to stay with my mother-in-law.

About 130,000 public workers were laid off after the July 15th coup attempt, they were also banned from international travel. As it was very difficult and time-consuming for the pro-Erdogan government officials to prepare the lists of the people with travel bans, some people like us were able to leave the country in the early days. At least a third of all judges and prosecutors were replaced with pro-government people regardless of their merit, or lack thereof.

Time was passing by despite all the hardship and pain around. We were waiting for our son to get some consolation, to ease our pain and sorrow. Although his passport was issued, my wife's parents didn't bring him to us for two more months. They all had U.S. visas, so that was not the reason. They were trying to punish me by doing so. Finally, after long begging of my wife, they brought him to us in the end.

When we thought that we were relieved from the social pressure in Turkey, my mother-in-law had brought that pressure back to our home. We were living under the same roof but not talking to each other. She was fully convinced that I was a traitor and kept insulting me using every occasion she had.

Not much later, about a week into our son's arrival, my mother-in-law made the fur fly. She told me that I was a terrorist and had to leave her son's house. She added that I was a loser living in misery and that I had deserved what happened to me. I couldn't take it anymore so I stood up and walked to another room, yet she came in front of the door and continued to insult me for about an hour. I was trembling with anger. I had already lost everything, and now I was hearing all these insults. But it was even more upsetting and painful for me to not hear any single word of defense from my wife. I couldn't stand it anymore and left the house. It was early fall, the weather was getting cold during the nights. Without any coat on me, I walked around the streets for hours. I was literally looking for a spot to curl and sleep but was also trying not to draw too much attention since I did not have legal residency yet. I was afraid that someone might call the police. I walked around on the main street but could find neither a church nor a mosque to go inside. Since I did not have a car, I did not have the luxury to sleep in a car, either. Looked for a quiet and unnoticeable corner in a park but couldn't find any, then went near a place where they had put dumpsters, but raccoons had taken that spot already. I waited for a long time in the cold night and then returned to the house to pack my belongings.

After a couple of hours of sleep, I woke up early in the morning and packed up several pieces of clothes. When I had left Turkey, I had not taken with me too much stuff in order not to draw any suspicion in the airport. People were doing so many different things in the airports for not being labeled as a Hizmet follower. I heard a woman, who was a Hizmet volunteer, put a pack of cigarettes in her bag, thinking that it would help her to pass the checkpoints more easily since everyone knew that a Hizmet volunteer wouldn't even smoke cigarettes.

I was packing my stuff into an old backpack that my brother-in-law had thrown to the attic. I had used that backpack a few times earlier. My wife entered the room and as if she was a complete stranger, with cold eyes she told me, "But that's not your bag!" She could have said, "What are you doing? Don't go! Where are you going?" But no, she said: "That's not your bag!" Up until then, my life was already ruined, but at that moment my wife had hammered the final nail in the coffin. It felt as if time had stopped and all the traces of my past life got buried into deep darkness. Now I had lost it all. My heart was fluttering like a newborn's heart. I was now alone in this whole universe. My wife had forsaken me.

I had brought only three hundred dollars to America after I had lost everything I had in Turkey. That money was soon about to run out. When I left the house and the cold wind hit my face, I took some time to think about it all. People whom I had taken for family had wiped me off. I had no one. I dragged my trembling body as if pulling a sack of flour. The streets were full of people and cars, but they looked so far away in my loneliness. I was not able to process any information around in this pitch darkness. I didn't know anywhere to go and anybody to ask for help. I didn't have a car and having no car in America is like having no pulse. Would I ever recover from all this pain and sorrow? Would my dignity which they have crushed ever heal? Could I start a new life?

I knew that I had to find a place to rest. I needed a warm corner, where I could lie down, close my eyes and hide in dreams. There was a park nearby, so I walked there instinctively. Sitting on a bench I thought about my entire life. I was a pretty intelligent and risk-averse individual, the risks I had taken in life were all calculated risks. But then, why was I in this situation now? What was it that I had done wrong? It was feeling as if someone behind me pushed me into a deep dark well, so deep that there was no light at all. I was literally a homeless person now. A person without a firm belief might behave differently in such a state. When a person is unfairly labeled as a terrorist without any reason or evidence, when he lost his everything and has nothing else left to lose, that person can be quite dangerous. But I had something which I had not lost yet. That was my belief in God. My heart was screaming and begging: "O Lord! Show me a path to salvation."

It was time for noon prayer. I was also hungry, so I entered a store to get water and something to eat. For the first time in my life, my bag was searched while exiting the store. I wondered why they had picked me while many others were exiting without being searched. Maybe my desperation and weakness were so obvious from the way I looked.

I performed the noon prayer in a park, under curious looks of people passing by. It was not an actual park, an open field rather, with a couple of trees around. Shortly after, I saw my wife and her mother walking nearby. When my wife saw me in the park, she approached. My mother-in-law did not even bother to look. I still had a little hope that my wife might say a few words of encouragement and perhaps apologize on behalf of her mother, but she only said: "Are we getting divorced?" Upon hearing that, I just stood frozen. Apparently, there are always worse things waiting when you think that you have seen the most terrible thing. Only a few months ago, I had a respectable status in society and a successful career. Then, all of a sudden, I was declared a terrorist and traitor. In order not to get imprisoned, I left my home country, only to become an undocumented immigrant here. No job, no permit, not even a driver's license, no place in this new society. And what was worse was that my life partner had forsaken me. I was even more desperate than being homeless because I didn't know how to live on the streets.

My wife left me there, just like that. That day was the turning point in my life. I had hit rock bottom. I walked around the park and tried to find a place to sleep at night. It was time for the afternoon prayer so I performed that. I kneeled down and sat so humble in front of my Lord. I felt as if I was cleansed from all the worldly things and purified. I was as pure as an unborn baby. All the worldly and material causes had gone silent for me.

Later, an idea popped into my hand. A few days ago, I had come across with a lawyer friend I knew from Turkey and got his phone number. We didn't know each other so well, but there was nothing else I could do. I called him and thankfully he came shortly after to pick me up from the park, carried my backpack, and brought me to his home. I felt both ashamed and grateful. Later I asked him: "Why all these happened to us?" He looked at me with a bitter smile. There were many questions unanswered, but one thing was clear: That coup was real, and it was made against the innocent people, like us.

FROM STREETS TO PALACE

My lawyer friend who opened the doors of his home to me probably will not know how big a favor this was for me. But my heart and my God knows that well. When I was left alone on the streets, him opening the doors of his home was beyond appreciation, it had meant the world to me. His apartment was pretty small. Most of the houses in the city were very expensive. Refugees like us were lucky if they could land in a small unit. In their apartment, they only had beds and a couple of dishes, that was it. They gave their older child's bed to me that night. May God host them in the palaces of Heaven! Just like me, they had also escaped from Turkey, with great difficulties. They had arrived here earlier than me, so they already had made several friends around the city. I was no longer a lonely outcast here. I stayed together with them for a few days. Then I moved into the basement of a house where college students were living. The walls in the basement were all cracked and there was a heavy odor due to humidity, not to mention the mice around. But I felt like I was living in a palace there. I was extremely happy and grateful to live in that basement because my second-best option was living on the streets. Imagine you are in the middle of a desert and almost dying from thirst, and you are offered a glass of water. Living together with people whom I can talk to and who would understand me was indeed a blessing, given the circumstances. I was feeling my heart beating again. There was light at the end of the tunnel.

I stayed in that house for a while and started to visit a business platform established by Hizmet affiliated businesspeople. As I was well-experienced with business associations back in Turkey, I tried to contribute with my time and expertise. One of my friends that I newly made took me even to psychological therapy on certain days. This was a time period of epiphany for me and people like me who had lost their everything. I have learned what real friendship meant. The real friend was the one who would give a hand at your moment of despair. The real wealth was your freedom and honor. Life was teaching us those lessons the hard way.

After some time, I collected my thoughts a bit and started to look for a job. About three months after being kicked out of my brother-in-law's house I started to work in a marble factory. I worked there for two years in many different positions, from production to sales to accounting. My hands and face were usually covered with marble dust, but my heart and conscious were clean. When I was leaving that job, we had a record revenue. I was able to put aside some money. I was planning to buy a car and was referred to someone who was selling his car. It was an old car, from 1994. I asked him if he could go ahead with a payment plan and he accepted. He was asking for $2,500 and that was above my budget. I tried to bargain, but he insisted on the same amount. Somehow, I suddenly burst into tears. That was not usual for me at all, but all that trauma I had been going through had made me so weak. Then he said: "No problem, you can pay whenever you have money, anytime." That gave me a relief as the thought of owing someone a debt and not being able to pay it was a big burden for me.

I was so happy that I finally had a car. Right after getting the car, I drove to the neighborhood where my wife was living. I had not seen my son for weeks. I called my wife and asked her to come out with my son so I could talk to her and see my son. I didn't want to ring the doorbell just in case my wife's mother would open the door and I really didn't want to see her mother. When my wife came out to the street, she looked down on my car and did not even bother to get in the car. She probably despised how old the car was. After the luxurious life in Istanbul, she was taking such things as an offense. For me, on the other hand, it was not a big deal. She talked to me very formal and cold. I hugged my son for a long time and then said to my wife that everything would be all right and we would go back to the good old days. I just wanted to see a glimpse of a smile on her face, but she was standing in front of me, ice-cold.

After a couple of months, I rented a partially furnished two-bedroom apartment at a quite reasonable price. I convinced my wife and brought her and my son from my brother-in-law's house to my apartment to live with me together. Despite all that had happened, I was trying to fix our family life. Honestly, I was trying mostly for the sake of our son.

I work for a law firm now, as of 2019, as a consultant and translator. Working in a job related to my profession is like a medicine for me. I see myself like a person trying to fix the damages after a hurricane hit his house. The path in front of me is long and full of hardships. I am preparing for the U.S. bar exams to get a lawyer license. In the meantime, I am trying to voluntarily support the purge victims of Turkey in their judicial affairs. Thank God, we make a living somehow. I help and advise people who had to leave the oppression in Turkey so that they will not live the hardships I had gone through before. Many lives have turned upside down with the staged so-called coup, unfortunately.

CLOTHES MAKE THE MAN

Most of the people I left behind in Turkey cut their ties with me. Many do not want to endanger their jobs in public offices by having contact with someone like me. I have saved myself and my family, but the purge fire is raging in Turkey. People I left behind seem weirdly to be determined to stay in that fire, but they don't want to burn, either!

When I had first come to America, I had felt like a fish out of water. Then I thought how a person when he dies, leaves all his wealth, his loved ones, and his friends behind. The dead would pass into an unknown realm and could not return to his old life anymore even if he wanted to. So how was my situation any different than that? I was like dead when I came here. I had died before the real death. I had lost my family, my friends, my wealth, my status, my titles…I lost them all and they all left me. My phone used to ring all the time before and I had a wide social circle. I had friends from all walks of life and all types of ideologies. After I came to America, only three people called me, only three…not a single person more.

There is an arrest warrant on me in Turkey now. A court ruled that I am a member of the terrorist (!) organization "FETO". I was supposedly trying to infiltrate the government to take it over for the so-called "Parallel State Structure"! Yeah, sure! You have to just laugh! If I were a part of any plan like that, I wouldn't have quitted my career in government years ago, in the first place.

My name is mentioned in some other court case files as well, but due to the confidentiality of the investigations, I don't know exactly how. In short, I am a wanted "terrorist" since some people saw it fit to do so! The judiciary process is ongoing, well of course if one can call it justice! I would call this a witch hunt, nothing else. I console myself with the hope to face those people in a fair and just court. The truth will ultimately prevail.

I will settle accounts with them in a real court one day. They didn't steal only my future, but also the future of my son. They didn't slander me only, but also my innocent son. These days will pass, but their cruel crimes will not be forgotten. The evil they have committed will backfire them and like a snake they fed and grew, it will bite them. That has been the unchanging rule of the world, whether you call it karma or the Eternal Justice of God. Fascism may find shelter in human's mind for some time but not for long. It is the goodness and kindness that is everlasting, no matter how weak they look or sound sometimes.

I am extremely sad for my country. Not because of its failing economy, or this or that... What I feel sad for are the values and virtues people of this nation have lost recently. This time period we are passing through proved that nothing is left from the legendary wisdom and insight that we believed Anatolian people had. I had not noticed how degenerated the ethical values were in Turkish society up until now. Being a patriot, I had overestimated that nation. I now see that it was all a big lie. I honestly think that Turkey is not worth the time and resources of the Hizmet movement.

When I was living abroad years ago with a respectable status in society, I had returned to Turkey in order to be beneficial to the people of my homeland. It has always been one of my priorities in life to help my countrymen. I now think that it was all in vain. I wish I had not returned years ago to Turkey and stayed in France. But then again, whatever I did, I did it for the sake of pleasing God, so I know that I shouldn't have any regret. Yet, I am only human and can't control sometimes the flames of reproach burning in me.

In retrospect, I now realize that I was pretty expendable in my home country. People greeting me respectfully when they entered my office, hundreds of contacts in my phone's address book… nothing was real. It was my social and economic status they had respected and cared for, not me. Here in America, I feel that I am valuable as a human being even if I don't have any wealth. My opinion and voice matters, rule of law is upheld and applied fairly and equally to all. May God bless this country and its people. I have been to many different countries, but America and its people are so special. I am very happy to be here with my family and so hopeful for my son's future. Thank God, we got rid of the evil of the corrupted society in Turkey. My son will grow in a civilized society where justice is respected. God-willing, if we can provide him a good education, he will be a modern, intellectual citizen and a good Muslim.

I must pass a crucial exam to be able to work as a lawyer in America, and for that, I must study very hard. I also aspire going to law school to get a master's degree. It's a long road in front of me, but worthwhile to walk along. The only remedy for someone who lost all is having new goals, and I have my goals, thankfully.

I grew up as a kid in poverty. The financial hardships were unsettling, but it was my emotional losses which tore me down. Currently, I don't want to remember anything related to my past in Turkey. That country does not exist as far as I am concerned. I care only for the innocent people and a few loved ones who are stuck living there.

I've lived through some terrible things in my life, but none of it was my choice. Alas! What's done is done. Our lives turned upside down. It's attributed to Rumi that he said: *"Instead of resisting to changes, surrender. Let life be with you, not against you. If you think that your life will be upside down, don't worry. How do you know down is not better than upside?"* I totally agree with that. All the traumas I had gone through were within the knowledge of my Lord. I know He won't do anything wrong or in vain. I also have faith that my life will only get better. How do I know that? Because I am able to see certain truths now, which I was blind of before. I am a more conscious Muslim. Now I see that my ideals as vast as embracing the entire humanity should not have been squeezed within the tight borders of Turkey, anyhow. I was living in a lie there. Rather than being the sultan of the palace of lies, I would prefer being the servant of the simple truth. As a world citizen, I am fully enthusiastic to contribute to the ideal of "The good and the beauty to prevail in the entire world."

THE END

AST PUBLISHING

  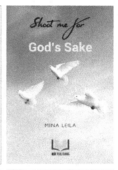